A Woman's Journey through

1 Peter

8 Lessons on Confidence
Exclusively for Women

Chariot Victor Publishing
A Division of Cook Communications

Titles by Dee Brestin

From Chariot Victor

The Friendships of Women
The Friendships of Women Workbook
We Are Sisters
The Joy of Women's Friendships
The Joy of Eating Right
The Joy of Hospitality
A Woman of Joy
A Woman of Value
A Woman of Insight
A Woman's Journey through Luke
A Woman's Journey through Ruth
A Woman's Journey through Esther
A Woman's Journey through 1 Peter
My Daughter, My Daughter

Fisherman Bible Study Guides

(Harold Shaw Publishers)
Proverbs and Parables
Ecclesiastes
Examining the Claims of Christ (John 1–5)
1, 2 Peter and Jude
How Should a Christian Live? (1, 2, 3 John)
Higher Ground
Building Your House on the Lord
Friendship

From Moody Press

Believer's Lifesystem—Women's Edition Bible Study

Chariot Victor Publishing
A division of Cook Communications, Colorado Springs, Colorado 80918
Cook Communications, Paris, Ontario
Kingsway Communications, Eastbourne, England

Unless otherwise noted, all Scripture quotations are from the *Holy Bible: New International Version*®. Copyright © 1973, 1978, 1984 by International Bible Society. Used by permission of Zondervan Publishing House. All rights reserved. Other quotations are from the *Holy Bible*, New Living Translation (NLT), Copyright © 1996 by Tyndale Charitable Trust. Used by permission of Tyndale House Publishers, Wheaton, IL 60189. All rights reserved; J.B. Phillips: *The New Testament in Modern English*, Revised Edition (PH), © J.B. Phillips, 1958, 1960, 1972, permission of Macmillan Publishing Co. and Collins Publishers; *The Message* (TM), Copyright © 1993. Used by permission of NavPress Publishing House; *The Living Bible* (TLB), © 1971, Tyndale House Publishers, Wheaton, IL 60189. Used by permission; and the *King James Version* (KJV) of the Bible.

Editors: Dorian Coover-Cox and Greg Clouse
Design: Bill Gray
Cover Photo: Image Bank

Contents

Our life on earth is filled with trials, temptations, and snares. Peter calls us to set our hope on God and thereby to live holy lives, to realize that we are just passing through this earth to our real eternal home. This is the central message of 1 Peter. *Pilgrim's Progress,* a marvelous allegory by John Bunyan, helps us to visualize Peter's

wilderness epistle. The above illustration by Robert Lawson is an overview of
Pilgrim's Progress. Christian makes the journey first. Later, his wife Christiana and
the children come to their senses and journey too. How do they face trials confidently?
They look ahead to the hope set before them.

How I Thank God For:

My Editors:
Dorian Coover-Cox of Dallas Theological Seminary, who has advised me with knowledge, discernment, and a true servant heart. She helped me see the theme of confidence in 1 Peter.

Greg Clouse, of Chariot Victor Publishing, whom I trust and respect.

My Assistant:
Gay Tillotson, who has the radiation Peter talks about—the steady beat of hope, hope, hope. She breezes into work each morning with excitement to comb the libraries, a manuscript, or to intercede in prayer.

My Prayer Team:
How I wish I could name each of you—but I give thanks upon every remembrance of you. Oh, the power of intercessory prayer!

My Family, Including:
All of our children, but especially our daughters at home: Beth and Anne.

Especially and always, my dear husband Steve, whose love for *Pilgrim's Progress* first inspired me. We are coheirs traveling toward the Celestial City. May we ever set our hope fully on the grace to be given us when Jesus Christ is revealed (1 Peter 1:13).

The Faithful and Gifted Servants of *Pilgrim's Progress:*
John Bunyan, for the wonderful gift of *Pilgrim's Progress*.
The illustrators who keep Bunyan's words vivid in our memories:
Robert Lawson, George Cruikshank, R.H. Brock, Randolph Klassen, E.F. Brewtnall, and F. Barnard.

Introduction

Confidence. Are you assured and gentle—or easily rattled? Do you walk through life with the steady beat of hope, hope, hope? Do you have the Spirit-filled radiation that causes others to ask the reason for the hope within you? Do you know the secret of genuine confidence?

Peter learned the secret as he walked with Jesus and now shares it in his first letter. It has to do with our focus, with grasping that this life is but a short preparation for our eternal home. The troubles we have, whether they are small, such as a colicky baby or an unfair boss, or large, such as breast cancer, a challenging marriage, or persecution for our faith, need not undo us. If we truly grasped the reality of the land to which we are journeying and the unfailing love and wisdom of the all-powerful God at our side, we would be filled with confidence, even in the midst of intimidation, and with an inextinguishable joy, even in the midst of sorrow. We are, Peter says, "aliens and strangers in the world" (2:11). We have been called to another country, to eternal glory, and this earth is simply a time to help us become, not happy, not comfortable, not rich— but like Jesus. First Peter is "a wilderness epistle." We are strangers on earth. As we pass through, we will face trials and they will increase as the end draws near. We need to learn *how* to face them with confidence.

While imprisoned for his faith, John Bunyan wrote an allegory that was to impact the world profoundly. Released in 1678, *Pilgrim's Progress* soon was outsold by only one book: the Bible itself. The story begins when Christian realizes his city is doomed for destruction. He tries to warn his wife and children to flee the wrath to come, but they think he has lost his mind. So he sets out alone, with an enormous burden on his back. When he reaches the cross, the burden tumbles down and joy fills his heart. Yet his sojourn has just begun. As he travels toward his real home in heaven, he faces temptations, valleys, and skeptical friends. How does he face them? By setting his hope in God! *The key to living confidently is to set your hope in God, who loves you and has called you for a purpose.*

Nestled within the letter of 1 Peter is a section directed only to women. Peter begins by speaking to those early Christian wives who came to Christ and were facing persecution from unbelieving husbands. Then he broadens his scope to all women, telling them how to live lives filled with hope. As we have done before in the *Woman's Journey* series, we will slow down and look very carefully at this section—a section which has often been misunderstood and misapplied. The light you will discover can transform your life and your marriage.

Special Instructions for Preparation and Discussion

Homework

In speaking across the country I am seeing a genuine hunger for in-depth Bible studies. The *Woman's Journey* series is divided into six daily thirty-minute quiet times. If you are overwhelmed on a particular day, you can take a shortcut by doing just the questions with asterisks.

These shortcuts will cause you to miss some wonderful views, but they are provided so that you do not give up on those frantic days (when the baby has a fever or you have a final exam). However, as you will discover if you read *Pilgrim's Progress*, don't take the shortcut because of sloth, for it will then lead to a much longer, more difficult road.

These lessons can be discussed in ninety minutes. If you don't have that much time, you have two options:

1.   Do the whole lesson but discuss half the questions. (I prefer this as it increases your time in the Word. But some groups, such as young moms, may find this overwhelming.)
2.   Do three days a week and stretch your study to sixteen weeks.

If you are new to Bible study, the best way to establish a habit is to choose the same time and the same place each day and stick to it. As a young Christian I would not allow myself to read or watch anything before I'd had my time with the Lord. Soon it wasn't a discipline but a desire.

Discussion

Imagine traveling with someone who talked your ear off—or, someone who was totally unresponsive. If you are naturally talkative, discipline yourself to speak not more than four times. If you are naturally shy, mark places where you will speak up, at least twice. If you have not done your homework, then allow the others to share and add only when they seem to be finished.

Make yourself vulnerable as the Lord leads. Women who are unwilling to be honest sacrifice bonding and growth. During the prayer time, confess areas in which you are struggling to live wholeheartedly for God. Get prayer support to break those strongholds—don't just ask for prayer for your Aunt Isabel's arthritis! Ask for prayer to fall more in love with Jesus and His Word. Keep confidences within the group.

Pilgrim's Progress, Pajamas, and Popcorn

Because illustrations and quotations from *Pilgrim's Progress* are laced through this study, plan a girls'-night-out sometime in the first month of your study. There are many versions of this classic available through interlibrary loan. Your local Christian bookstore may have a video version of *Pilgrim's Progress*, as there are several. *Dangerous Journey*, a beautiful version, is available in both book and video. The video can be obtained from Gateway Video: 1-800-523-0226. A version of the book with especially lovely illustrations is *Pilgrim's Progress* retold by Mary Godolphin (published by Frederick Stokes, illustrated by Robert Lawson). After viewing the video or reading a children's illustrated version, have a time of discussion, allowing each woman to share a few highlights and how they might be relevant to her life. This will not only help you to know your sisters better, but it will help you to understand the big picture of 1 Peter. You can do this anytime during the study, but if you do it soon it will have the added benefit of giving everyone an overview. Not ready to wear pajamas together? Then just come in casual clothes. I would also encourage you to read *Pilgrim's Progress*, either individually or to your family. A good modern translation is *Pilgrim's Progress in Today's English* (retold by James H. Thomas, Moody Press).

Christian, feeling his load of sin, breaks out with a lamentable cry. He must begin the journey alone, leaving his family in the city doomed to destruction.

One

Strangers on Earth

This week you will be preparing for the journey. You will get to know your traveling companions (if you are doing this in a small group), you will meet your guide (Peter), and you will look over your itinerary, for you will get a glimpse of some of the key themes in 1 Peter.

Memory Work

Peter says "Prepare your minds for action" (1:13). To do this, we will be memorizing Scripture. Don't throw up your hands and say, "But I can't memorize!" Even if you have failed in the past, here is a plan that has helped many: take it a word at a time, a few words a day. If you spend just a minute a day, you will be amazed at what you will accomplish in eight weeks. On pages 133–34 at the back of this guide you will find all of the memory passages. Photocopy or tear out the page and put it on your bathroom mirror or your dashboard. If you have a screen saver on your computer, type your verse there. Be faithful, not only to yourself, but as an example to the sisters in your small group. Each week you will have a required passage **(in bold print)** and an extra credit passage (in regular print).

> [3]**Praise be to the God and Father of our Lord Jesus Christ! In his great mercy he has given us new birth into a living hope through the resurrection of Jesus Christ from the dead,** [4]*and into an inheritance that can never perish, spoil or fade—kept in heaven for you,* [5]*who through faith are shielded by God's power until the coming of the salvation that is ready to be revealed in the last time. (1 Peter 1:3-5)*

Warm-Up

Tell your name and a sentence about yourself. Then share, in a phrase, a feeling you recall when you were "a stranger" in a new city, new church, or new Bible study.

Day 1: Instructions for the Journey

The opening introductions are vital. Read them carefully.

*1.   Comment on what stood out to you from :

   *A. The Introduction (pp. 7–8).

   *B. The Special Instructions for Preparation and Discussion (pp. 9–10).

2.   Spend a minute or a few minutes on the memory passage.

Praise

Praise be

Praise be to. . .

3.   Read through the short book of 1 Peter in a standard translation such as the *New International Version* or the *New American Standard Bible*. Whenever you see the word *stranger*, highlight it.

Day 2: Where Am I Going?

Today you will read through the Book of 1 Peter more carefully. As you read, look not only at the verses that have the actual word *stranger* in them, but those which have the concept of passing through this difficult wilderness of earth to our eternal home in heaven with Christ.

Prepare your heart by singing "Surely Goodness and Mercy" (p. 138) on your own.

4.   When you find a verse or section with the *concept*, record the reference, the passage, and a summary of it in your own words. I've done one in chapter 1 as a model for you. Choose just one passage (though there are several) in each chapter, including one of your own in chapter 1.

A. 1 Peter 1

1 Peter 1:6-7: In this you greatly rejoice, though now for a little while you may have had to suffer grief in all kinds of trials. These have come so that your faith—of greater worth than gold, which perishes even though refined by fire—may be proved genuine and may result in praise, glory and honor when Jesus Christ is revealed.

Summary: On earth I will go through trials, but like fire that refines gold, those trials will prove that my faith is genuine. That refined faith will result in praise at the end of my journey when Jesus is revealed.

*Your turn:

*B. 1 Peter 2 (Find a verse directed to you as a stranger, write it out, and summarize it.)

C. 1 Peter 3 (As women who are sojourners on earth, we should value what is permanent rather than the transitory. Find a verse about this, write it out, and summarize it.)

D. 1 Peter 4 (Find a verse that describes the right attitude toward suffering that a stranger on earth should have. Write it out and summarize it.)

E. 1 Peter 5 (Find a verse that particularly speaks to you today as you travel as a stranger on earth. Write it out and summarize it.)

Memory Work

Continue your memorization of 1 Peter 1:3 (verse on p. 13).

Day 3: Getting to Know the Young Peter

The Apostle Peter is your guide. How he models what he writes! In his preface to 1 Peter, Eugene Peterson observes:

> From what we know of the early stories of Peter, he had in him all the makings of a bully. That he didn't become a bully (and religious bullies are the worst kind) but rather the boldly confident and humbly self-effacing servant of Jesus Christ that we discern in these letters, is a compelling witness to what he himself describes as "a brand-new life, with everything to live for." [1]

Today you will study the young Peter. He was confident, but that confidence was in himself, in his own strength. Tomorrow you will study a humbled, commissioned, and transformed Peter. Because of his responsiveness to his tests and trials during his journey on earth, Peter became the man God had called him to be. Instead of trusting in himself, Peter learned how to set his hope in Christ. This is the secret of an unshakable confidence, the kind which made Peter a rock.

*5.   Read Matthew 14:22-33 and describe what happened and the admirable quality you see in Peter in verses 28-29.

*What weakness do you see in Peter in this passage?

*How did Jesus rebuke him?

*How did Peter respond to the rebuke? (vv. 32-33)

One of the primary themes of 1 Peter is hope. It is not the way we use hope in contemporary English (I hope it will snow), but instead is similar to faith, meaning a confident expectation based on what we know to be true about God. As you page back in Matthew, what are some of the miracles to which Peter had been an eyewitness which should have helped him be confident in Christ?

*In your own life, what are some of the ways you have seen God's power and goodness? (List at least three specific ways.)

*Name one circumstance you are facing right now which could be frightening. How could your past experiences help you to trust God?

Cast all your anxiety on him because he cares for you (1 Peter 5:7).

6. Read Matthew 16:13-20. Describe Simon Peter's confession.

The pronouncement [of Jesus] can be read either seriously, as if to say, "You are indeed a strong foundation," or ironically, as if to say, "Some rock you are!" The section as a whole favors an ironic reading.[2]

Why do you think Jesus changed Simon's name to Peter? Is Jesus building His church on Peter or on Peter's confession of faith? Explain.

His given name was Simon, but Jesus changed it to Peter, which means "a stone" . . . often he is called "Simon Peter." Perhaps the two names suggest a Christian's two natures: an old nature (Simon) that is prone to fail, and a new nature (Peter) that can give victory. As Simon, he was only another human piece of clay; but Jesus Christ made a rock out of him!—Warren Wiersbe[3]

Following this, how did Peter show his feet of clay? (Matthew 16:21-23)

7.   Whom did Peter call the rock in 1 Peter 2:4-8?

In 1 Peter 2:9-11, how does Peter tell you to see yourself? How might grasping this lead to genuine confidence?

8.   What was Simon Peter privileged to witness in Matthew 17:1-8? (Another theme of 1 Peter is Christ's glory. Peter got a glimpse here!)

What error did Simon Peter make? How did God correct him?

How did Peter use this experience for good? (See 2 Peter 1:16-18.)

*9.   Read John 18:1-11 and Matthew 26:47-54. What error did Simon Peter make here? How did Jesus rebuke him?

*Another theme in 1 Peter is that God is the sovereign judge. Even when we face unfair treatment we can have confidence, for God will be our judge. Read 1 Peter 2:19-23 and describe Peter's changed perspective.

*10. Is there a situation in your life where you are being treated unfairly? How could you learn from 1 Peter 2:19-23?

Memory Work
Spend a minute continuing your memorization of 1 Peter 1:3.

Day 4: The Transformed Peter
We love Peter for his bold enthusiasm, but perhaps the quality that Jesus loved most was his teachable heart. Our Lord talked to him more than any of the other disciples, rebuked him the hardest, and praised him the most. Peter learned his lessons during his journey through earth. He lived a blazing, confident faith and died a martyr's death.

Tradition says Peter was crucified upside-down, for he did not feel worthy to die as his Lord had died. This relief is in Rome, Italy.

*11. Read Matthew 26:69-75 and describe Peter's failure and repentance.

What evidence do you find of God's reinstatement of Peter in Mark 16:7?

What did Peter learn from his failure? (1 Peter 3:13-15)

12. Read John 21:1-17. List all the ways Jesus showed love toward Peter.

In speaking to the Christian Booksellers Association convention in Dallas, R.C. Sproul spoke on this passage and pleaded with owners of Christian bookstores to offer "milk" for beginners and "meat" for the rest, but to keep the junk food out.[4] That was quite a challenge, as junk food sells! I believe we need to take this challenge to heart as well, for ourselves, and for our children. God has appointed you, if you are a mother, as guardian over the minds of your growing children. This guide encourages you to read Pilgrim's Progress—*a classic every Christian should read. Get a copy this week!*

What prophecy did Jesus give Peter in John 21:18-19?

13. Sometimes it is helpful to know the journey to heaven may be rough. What instructions did Peter give in 1 Peter 4:12-13?

14. The Book of Acts shows us Peter, a mighty man of God who preached the first sermon at Pentecost (Acts 2), performed the first miracle (Acts 3), and much more. Read Acts 2:14-4:22 and record several phrases that show the boldness and faith of the transformed Peter.

*15. Consider some of the failures in your life. Have you learned from them? If so, give evidence.

*Consider some of the trials in your life. Was your faith proved genuine? If so, what did you believe about God which gave you confidence?

Memory Work
Review 1 Peter 1:3.

Day 5: Making This Journey Come Alive!

As a child my parents took me on some wonderful trips abroad, yet I remember the swimming pools better than the cathedrals and catacombs. As I matured I studied the history before we traveled, and it made all the difference. Likewise, an understanding of the situation of the early Christians will make 1 Peter come alive.

Peter wrote this letter at a time of savage persecution against Christians. On July 19, A.D. 64, Rome was burned and citizens blamed the emperor, Nero. Needing a scapegoat, Nero had Christians arrested, blaming them for the fire. This led to widespread martyrdom.

> Their deaths were made farcical. Dressed in wild animals' skins, they were torn in pieces by dogs, or crucified, or made into torches to be ignited after dark as substitutes for daylight. Nero provided his gardens for the spectacle.[5]

One of the most difficult theological questions has to do with how a loving God can allow His children to suffer such horrors. This is an important question. Many believers are being martyred today. Many also feel that the attitude in the free world toward evangelical Christians is changing from ridicule to persecution. Are you ready?

Personal Assignment:

Imagine persecution coming to you or your children. Read through 1 Peter in a paraphrase (*Phillips*, the *New Living Translation*, or *The Message*). Star the verses that tell how we should respond to persecution.

Another way to make this journey come alive is by understanding the rich history of *Pilgrim's Progress* and looking carefully at the illustrations in this guide, which are from artists from the 17th century to the present. Look carefully at the details and you'll be surprised what you discover.

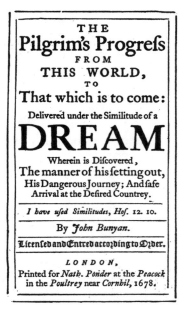

THE
Pilgrim's Progreſs
FROM
THIS WORLD,
TO
That which is to come:
Delivered under the Similitude of a
DREAM
Wherein is Diſcovered,
The manner of his ſetting out,
His Dangerous Journey; And ſafe
Arrival at the Deſired Countrey.

I have uſed Similitudes, Hoſ. 12. 10.

By *John Bunyan.*

Licenſed and Entred according to Order.

LONDON,
Printed for *Nath. Ponder* at the *Peacock*
in the *Poultrey* near *Cornbil,* 1678.

Above is the title-page of the original edition of *The Pilgrim's Progress.*
The letters that look to us like "ſ" show an old way of making the letter "s."

Memory Work
Review 1 Peter 1:3.

Day 6: Getting to Know Your Traveling Companions
God has blessed women with a gift for intimacy. You are going to have an opportunity in this study to get to know each other soul-to-soul. Of the following four descriptions, choose the one that comes closest to describing the start of your spiritual journey. Then write one sentence (and one sentence only) describing your journey's start. (You will be given the freedom to pass.) Be prepared to share your sentence in closing at the first study or, if your group is planning a pajama party soon, you could do it then and share in greater depth (several sentences each).

*17. Which of the following descriptions comes closest to yours?
A. Like Timothy, I came to know Christ as a little child and have never been far away from Him.

B. Like Paul, I came to know Christ when I was older in a dramatic conversion experience.

C. Like Timothy, I came to know Christ as a child—but I fell far from Him and rededicated my life when I was older.

D. I have not yet put my trust in Christ, but I may be on the way.
Which comes closest? Write one sentence summarizing your story here:

Memory Work
Review 1 Peter 1:3.

Prayer Time
This guide will lead you gently into various prayer exercises. Today stand in a circle and hold hands. Moving clockwise, each woman will bless the woman on her right with one short sentence. She may say something like "Thank You Lord for giving Dawn her gentle spirit." If she doesn't know Dawn, she can say, "Lord, please bless Dawn." If she doesn't want to pray audibly, she can pray silently and squeeze Dawn's hand so that Dawn knows it is her turn.

Two

The Purpose of
Our Earthly Journey

*J*oni Eareckson Tada has had more than thirty years in a wheelchair to consider the problem of pain. Her powerful book *When God Weeps* (coauthored with Steven Estes) makes some amazing statements that you will find corroborated in 1 Peter (and *Pilgrim's Progress*).

First, despite Christ's compassionate death for our sins, God's plan—not plan B or C or D, but his plan—calls for all Christians to suffer, sometimes intensely. To encourage us, he may write some light moments into the script of our lives—he may include adventure or romance. An amusing situation will get us chuckling, an occasional twist of plot may delight us to tears, for God loves to give. But without fail, some scenes are going to break your heart. . . .

Second, God's plan is specific. . . .He doesn't reach for a key, wind up nature with its sunny days and hurricanes, then sit back and watch the show. He doesn't let Satan prowl about totally unrestricted. . . . He's not our planet's absent landlord. Rather, he screens the trials that come to each of us—allowing only those that accomplish his good plan, because he takes no joy in human agony.

Third, the core of his plan is to rescue us from our sin. Our pain, poverty, and broken hearts are not his ultimate focus. He cares about them, but . . . God cares most— not about making us comfortable—but about teaching us to hate our sins, grow up spiritually, and love him.[6]

When we come to Christ, He makes us holy in the sight of God. But holiness is also an ongoing process. Trials don't automatically make us holy, but when we set our hope on the grace to be given when Christ is revealed, we become holy, as He is holy. As this occurs we also grow in confidence—both now, and a confidence that we will be unashamed before Christ at His coming.

One of the keys of confidence is to continually set our hope in Christ and to look ahead to "an inheritance incorruptible" (1 Peter 1:4, KJV). We must persist on the narrow road, setting our hope on Jesus. In *Pilgrim's Progress*, Christian's neighbors, Pliable and Obstinate, chase after him to leave the narrow road and return to the comforts of home. Christian says:

> *"That can never be. You dwell in the City of Destruction. Be convinced, good neighbors, and go along with me."*

> *"What!" exclaimed Obstinate. "And leave all our friends and comforts behind?"*

> *"Yes," said Christian (for that was his name), "for all that you seek is not worthy to be compared to . . . an inheritance incorruptible and undefiled, that will never fade away, safely laid up in Heaven, to be bestowed at the appointed time to all who diligently seek it. Read it, if you will, right here in my book."*
> *(1 Peter 1:4)*

> *Obstinate: "Oh, bosh! Away with your book! Will you go back with us or not?"[7]*

Memory Work

Review last week's passage. (All passages are printed on pages 133–134.)
If you didn't memorize last week, begin fresh with this week's verse in bold.
Extra credit? Do 1 Peter 1:6 as well.

> *[6]In this you greatly rejoice, though now for a little while you may have had to suffer grief in all kinds of trials. [7]These have come so that your faith—of greater worth than gold, which perishes even though refined by fire—may be proved genuine and may result in praise, glory and honor when Jesus Christ is revealed. (1 Peter 1:6-7)*

Warm-Up

Can you think of a trial you faced with genuine confidence? In one breath, what was it and what did you believe about God which strengthened you?

Day 1: Overview

*1. What stood out to you from the introduction to this lesson?

Read through 1 Peter 1.

2. What impressed you in this reading?

3. Peter uses many phrases which would trigger memories to his recipients of another journey, that of the Israelites from slavery into freedom.

A. Compare Exodus 12:1-13 with:

For you know that it was not with perishable things such as silver or gold that you were redeemed from the empty way of life handed down to you from your forefathers, but with the precious blood of Christ, a lamb without blemish or defect. (1 Peter 1:18-19)

What parallel do you see?

B. Compare Exodus 12:11 with:
Wherefore gird up the loins of your mind, be sober. (1 Peter 1:13a, KJV)
What parallel do you see?

C. Compare Exodus 24:4-8 with:
Who have been chosen . . . for obedience to Jesus Christ and sprinkling by his blood. (1 Peter 1:2)
What parallel do you see?

D. Compare Deuteronomy 12:9 with:
And into an inheritance that can never perish, spoil or fade—kept in heaven for you. (1 Peter 1:4)
What parallel do you see? What difference?

*4. Not only the Exodus generation, but continuing on through the generations, Israel showed a pattern. Find it in Psalm 78:9-20 (esp. v. 11).

*5. When we face trials, we need to remember God's character and goodness from the past and therefore "hope" (trust) in His promises for the future (1 Peter 1:13). How might you apply this to a concern you are facing right now?

Sing "Rock of Ages" (p. 137) in your quiet time.

The Slough of Despond is a place where the doubts and fears of sinners awakened by the Holy Spirit have settled. Both Pliable and Christian fall in. Pliable has had enough of seeking God and retreats to the City of Destruction, but Christian sets his hope on the joy set before him and persists through the slough to the other side where a new friend, Help, is there to pull him out.

Memory Work
Spend a minute memorizing 1 Peter 1:7 (p. 25).

Day 2: An Apostle Writing to Exiles
Peter began this letter by stating his credentials. He was an apostle. Read how he elaborated on this in his second epistle.

> *For we were not making up clever stories when we told you about the power of our Lord Jesus Christ and his coming again. We have seen his majestic splendor with our own eyes. And he received honor and glory from God the Father when God's glorious, majestic voice called down from heaven, "This is my beloved Son; I am fully pleased with him." We ourselves heard the voice when we were there with him on the holy mountain. (2 Peter 1:16-18, NLT)*

Having established his authority, Peter quickly turns his concern to his recipients who are scattered and facing persecution, and he offers words of assurance. *The Message* paraphrases 1 Peter 1:1-2 like this:

> *I, Peter, am an apostle on assignment by Jesus, the Messiah, writing to exiles scattered to the four winds. Not one is missing, not one forgotten. God the Father*

has his eye on each of you, and has determined by the work of the Spirit to keep you obedient through the sacrifice of Jesus. May everything good from God be yours.[8]

*6. Trials and troubles can make us feel forgotten by God. How does Peter assure the recipients of this letter?

How might you apply the above truth to a concern in your personal life?

Personal Action Assignment

Think about a trial your husband (or another loved one) is facing. Pray in faith for him, using 1 Peter 1:7. One way to pray confidently is to pray through Scripture, for that is always in God's will. Here's a model using the above passage.

Father, as my husband faces challenges working with a man in authority who seems unfair, I ask that You would anoint my husband with discernment, grace, and peace. May he trust in You and discover Your faithfulness. May this trial result in an even stronger faith, of greater worth than gold. And may this all result in praise, glory, and honor when Jesus Christ is revealed.

Read 1 Peter 1:1-2 in a standard translation.

7.   Each Person of the Trinity is involved in preparing believers for their journey through life.

   A. What does God the Father do?
   chooses us

Dale:
The plan

Election is a prominent scriptural theme and is much more than simply God's foreknowledge of our responses, for it is presented as an initiative of God. It is an important message as we face "the problem of pain." Nothing, as Joni Eareckson Tada says, slips through God's fingers without His permission. He has a plan for our lives, and that is to conform us to the image of Christ (Romans

8:29). He has also chosen those who will believe (Ephesians 1:11). How do you balance election with the other prominent scriptural theme of free will?
B.C. Caffin comments:

> The sacred writers seem to recognize the fact that we are in the presence of an insolvable mystery; and they teach us by their silence that the proper attitude of the Christian when brought face to face with the mystery, is rest in the Lord, humble child-like faith in his love and wisdom.[9]

B. What does God the Spirit do?

Sanctify

C. What does God the Son do?

*He was our sacrifice
We are to obey Him*

Memory Work
Spend a minute memorizing 1 Peter 1:7 (p. 25).

Day 3: These Trials Have Come to Test Faith
I've just come from speaking in Stone Mountain, Georgia where four churches worked together to put on a wonderful woman's seminar where God's Spirit was intensely present and many lives were changed. At a dinner for the committee the night before, I asked what they had learned from God. Together they told me, "To walk by faith." Fran, a perky brunette, elaborated:

> A few weeks before, the registration numbers just weren't coming in. We were in a panic. We'd done everything we could think to do. As we were praying, we realized we were doing this in our own strength and not trusting God. Our confidence had been in ourselves. We got down on our knees, weeping, repentant, telling Him we would walk by faith, we would put our confidence in Him.

How vital it is we learn this lesson. When Pilgrim is on his journey, he must pass between two lions. Frightened, he stops. But Watchful calls out to him:

"Is thy strength so small? Fear not the two wild beasts for they are bound by chains, and are put here to try the faith of those that have it, and to find out those that have none. Keep in the midst of the path and no harm shall come to thee."[10]

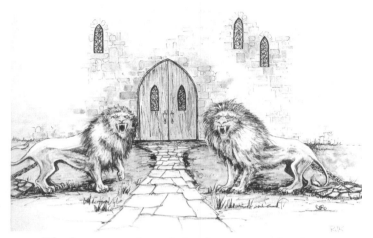

The lions were chained, but he saw not the chains.

It is hardest to trust God and keep on the path when the trials are intensely personal. We ask: "How can a loving God allow slander, a miscarriage, or a betraying husband?" He has the power to swoop down and stop it, so why, so often, doesn't He? The best answer we have is the one He gave Job, which you will consider today. Our vision is earthbound, myopic—but God can see eternity. God cares about our pain, but He has something far greater in mind than our ease or comfort. He wants for us a purified faith, a sanctified life, and a total salvation.

Read 1 Peter 1:3-9.

The Load Slid from his Back

At the cross, Christian's burden tumbles off, and he is born anew into a living hope through the resurrection of Jesus Christ from the dead.

*9. Explain how our salvation involves the past (v. 3), the present (v. 5), and the future (v. 4).

James 1:21

He has given us new hope

He shields - protects us Now

He gives us an inheritance...

*10. Have you received the new birth? If so, give some evidences. How would your life be different if you had not received Christ and if the Holy Spirit were not living in you?

11. How does the protection of believers take place? What is God's part, and what is our part? (v. 5)

We are shielded by God's power

We have faith.

Share a time when you trusted God in the midst of difficulty and sensed His presence and protection.

Th 2-21
pm

*12. What happens when we trust God in the midst of trials? (v. 7)

Our faith is proved genuine resulting in praise, honor & glory when Christ comes

*13. Hope, meaning "confident expectation," is a theme of 1 Peter, introduced here in verse 3. Meditate on that verse and look ahead to its uses in 1 Peter 1:13 and 3:15. Often, we set our hope on a change in our circumstances (If only my extended family could be less angry, if only I could have a baby. . .). What is the object of our hope in these passages?

1:13 God's grace given to us when Christ is revealed.
1:3 new hope in Christ's Res.
3:15 Jesus

14. When a trial comes and your circumstances are *not* changed, how can you still be okay? What is the secret, according to the above Scriptures?

Christ is our hope
God's mercy

One woman said: "I have come to realize that if God never 'fixes' my husband's drinking problem, I can still be okay."

Is there an application to your life? If so, what?

15. Job suffered intensely and wondered why. Read God's fascinating answer to him in Job 38–41. Write down the phrases that impress you and then summarize God's answer. *v.1 we ask about knowledge (How dare we question God)*

38 V.21 sarcasm
39:35 Do they report to you
cf 39:9 ff - who do we trust to provide...
CH 40: Do we dare contend with the Almighty correct the Almighty 40:8-14

How does Job 19:25 exemplify Peter's command in 1 Peter 1:3?

Hope Job had hope that his Redeemer lives - the same hope Peter speaks of

*16. Though God hurts with us in our pain and cares for us (see 1 Peter 5:7), there is something much more important to Him than our ease and comfort. What is it, according to 1 Peter 1:7, 9? *our faith, our salvation*

Memory Work
Spend a minute memorizing 1 Peter 1:7.
These have come so that your faith ... may be proved genuine and may result in praise, glory and honor when J.C. is revealed

Day 4: Prophets and Angels Longed to Understand

I was a young wife and mother when my sister Sally visited me in order to tell me about Jesus and urge me to trust Him with my whole life. But what if the Bible was simply a cluster of well-written fables? I didn't want to give up the worldly things I thought might fulfill me if Jesus was a fairy tale. Sally was making me uncomfortable and I was eager for her to return to Ohio. To my dismay, a blizzard delayed her departure. During that time Sally showed me prophecies in the Old Testament that pointed to the coming of Christ. Though David lived a thousand years before Christ and Isaiah seven hundred years before, both detailed exactly how Jesus would die. As the snow piled up outside our window, I read their prophecies with my sister, and the "Spirit of Christ," the same Spirit who spoke to the prophets long ago, the warm breath of the Lion of Judah, began to thaw my icy heart.

Peter tells us the prophets themselves longed to understand when their prophecies would be fulfilled. He also makes the intriguing statement that "even angels long to look into these things." The phrase, "look into" is a picturesque phrase meaning "peer over." Like humans, angels are not omniscient. If even angels are interested in this, how much more should we, to whom the good news has come, be longing to know more about it.

We will suffer on this earth, but that suffering, if we follow in the steps of Christ, will end in glory. You can see how Peter, in his life, finally came to understand suffering was part of God's plan. Though Peter was familiar with Old Testament prophets and their words about suffering and glory to come, he failed to grasp them. Then he witnessed the suffering of Jesus firsthand. He was confused, he was afraid—but he kept seeking. He witnessed the glory of the Transfiguration and finally the glory of the resurrected Christ. At Pentecost and again in his letters, we see an enlightened Peter, as the same "Spirit of Christ"

[handwritten: We have seen the fulfillment and confidence and to ...]
[handwritten: The prophets didn't see the fulfillment]

who thundered through the prophets thundered through this transformed
fisherman. Those who met him were astonished at his confidence (see Acts
4:13).

[handwritten: 8am 2-28-02]

Read 1 Peter 1:10-12.

*17. What did the prophets speak about? What was their attitude? (v. 10)

*[handwritten: They spoke of the grace that was to come.
They searched intently w/ greatest care to find the time
of Jesus predicted suffering and glorification]*

*What Spirit was in the prophets and what did He predict? (v. 11)

*[handwritten: "Spirit of Christ" was in them,
predicting His time of suffering then glory]*

*What did that Spirit reveal to the prophets? (v. 12)

*[handwritten: They were not serving themselves, but us.
- They were seeing pieces - we see the puzzle
more put together.]*

*Who else longs to understand these mysteries? (v. 12) What does this teach
you about these beings?

*[handwritten: Angels - even they don't have
the relationship of God through Jesus that
is available to us.]*

*18. What do you imagine the angels thought when they saw the humble
circumstances of Christ's birth? The degradation of the cross?

[handwritten: They must have wondered at God's ways - like we do, but with even more frustration]

19. In 1 Peter 1:11, Peter uses the phrase "the sufferings of Christ and the glories
that would follow." Read the following prophecies and describe the sufferings of
Christ and the following glory they predicted:

   A. Psalm 22 *[handwritten: forsaken by God, verbal 13, physical death 14]*

   *[handwritten: V.19 turns to praise
V.27 - all earth will bow down to Him]*

   B. Isaiah 53

   *[handwritten: V.12 give him a portion among the great
V.10 many children]*

Sufferings now, glories to follow. Peter wants to encourage Christians who face the first to look for the second. . . . Now he would have us remember that the Christ of glory is the Christ of the cross. . . . Likewise the message of the prophets pronounces God's judgment on the sin of his people, but it does not stop with judgment. The final vision of the Old Testament is not of dry bones in death valley. Rather, it is renewal beyond conceiving.[11]

*20. Look ahead to 1 Peter 2:21 and describe our calling.

follow in his steps

According to 1 Peter 2:22-23, how did Christ respond when He suffered? Find the secret to His amazing submissiveness in verse 23.

he did not retaliate, made no threats, He entrusted himself to Him who is just! God!

*21. Is there an unfair situation you are facing? How could you follow in Christ's steps?

Wed 9am

Memory Work
Continue memorizing 1 Peter 1:7.

Day 5: Therefore, Be Holy, as He Is Holy
I've been listening to messages by Dr. Stephen Olford on this letter. If you are familiar with Dr. Olford's preaching, try to imagine his booming voice, his rolling r's, his intensity! As if I were hearing the prophets of old, I hear the roar of "The Lion of Judah."

In a day of suffering? What is the answer? The yielded heart! Set apart Christ as Lord! You will never know victory, fullness of Spirit until Jesus Christ is unrivaled, undisputed, and unchallenged Lord!

Can you honestly say without reservation that He is:
Lord of every thought and action
Lord of my speaking, giving—Lord of all!
Lord of my friendships,

Lord of my love, courtship, marriage,
Lord of my business, money, pleasures,
Lord of my home, devotions, family altar,
Lord of my eating, praying, sleeping—Lord of all?

Is there any area in your life that is not surrendered? Is there any bridgehead the devil can use to bring you down? . . . From Genesis to Revelation God blazes out His message: Be ye holy as I am holy! The reason He has called us, predestined us, elected us—was that we be conformed to the image of Christ![12]

*22. How would you answer Dr. Olford's challenging questions?

Kids school, frustration w/ unsaved family

Read 1 Peter 1:13-16.

23. The word *prepare* (v. 13) conjured up the picture of people in biblical times tucking up their flowing robes for walking and running. (See 1 Kings 18:46.) Spiritually, we must also be unencumbered. Compare this to the word picture given in Hebrews 12:1. What do you see? *Getting rid of the extra garbage of life so we might live simply + free, unburdened, unhindered in*

Is there a sin encumbering you, keeping you from running well? Describe what your life might be without it?

our walk w/ God

24. We are to be "self-controlled." What do you learn from Peter's elaboration on this phrase in 4:7 and 5:8?

4:7 Be clear minded, so we can pray the end is near
5:8 Be alert, because Satan is around

How could you better apply this to your life?

Satan can blind us with ourself - look beyond self

25. What is the closing command of verse 13?

Set your hope fully on the grace given when J.C. is revealed

You show me a person who walks across the stage of life with a quiet certainty—not cockiness, but hope—and they're going to be followed by a thousand people.[13]

List some of the reasons you have to be hopeful as a believer.

26. How would you describe obedient children?

trusting, not questioning why, pleasure to be around, peaceful, confident, comfortable

What command is given in verse 14?

Don't conform - give in to - the evil desires we had while unknowing of God's grace. God is greater than the evil desires

What were some of the evil desires you had when you lived in ignorance?

Bad language, lust, coveteousness, deceitfullness selfishness

21st 9am home

Every Christian has a Spirit-filled vibration, a radiation. . . . What are some of the evidences of that radiation? The radiation of certainty—the hope, hope, hope—the beat of 1 Peter.[14]

27. Would those closest to you say that hope (confidence in Christ) and purity radiate from you?

*28. Put verses 15-16 in your own words.

God is holy, he loves me, called me, waits for me I desire His grace, I love him, while I wait for Him I will be holy.

Memory Work
Review your memory work.

Day 6: Live Your Lives as Strangers Here

Sometimes being holy can seem like a myriad of commands, but it is really quite simple. In *Pilgrim's Progress*, Christian asks Goodwill how he can be sure not to lose his way as he sojourns. Goodwill replies:

> There are many roads branching off from this one, but you can distinguish the right way from the wrong, for the right way is the only one that is straight and narrow.[15]

Read 1 Peter 1:17-25.

- obvious
- less traveled - following the
- not following crowd

29. How does Peter tell us to live our lives here? (v. 17) What does this mean to you? live as strangers here, since we call on a Heavenly Father. The ways of the world should seem unfair, unusual, not good, hopeless — strange!

How could you apply this to your life? I shouldn't be afraid to be shocked at the injustice, shocked at sin in my life. I should be willing to live by God's standards when they are in conflict w/the world's — wealth, material things.

30. Describe who redeemed us and how (vv. 18-21).
I am redeemed by the precious Blood of Jesus — the Lamb w/out blemish. Not by worldly perishable things — my hope should be wholely in Him — not stuff, house, car, clothes, bank account, etc

31. How is an ungodly heritage described in verse 18?
A heritage of perishable things — silver + gold even.

If you did not grow up in a godly home, what hope can you find here?
My heritage is not in what my parents leave me, but in what my heavenly Father has already given me.

32. How do we purify ourselves? (v. 22)
by obeying the truth — leading to sincere love for one another
by deeply loving each other

33. The Christian life is not difficult to understand. Here, Peter sums it up in one command. What is it? (v. 22b) *love one another deeply — from the heart*

In A Woman's Journey to the Heart of God, Cynthia Heald encourages us, as sojourners on earth, to travel light! Let go of the grudges, the hurts, and the bitterness that are so heavy, so cumbersome, and so draining![16]

April 18th

Personal Action Assignment

Are you holding onto any sins? Any grudges? Any past hurts? Kneel before God and imagine you are at the foot of the cross. One by one, lay each burden down. Then sing the "Cares Chorus" (see p. 135).

34. What do you learn about the word of God in verse 23? In verses 24-25?

It is living and enduring — lasting — imperishable. It stands forever — true forever.

*35. What do you think you will remember from this week's lesson?

p 35 — God's purpose for the prophets message was to benefit us — not them — there is always a bigger picture than just me

p 39 — I already have my inheritance — an everlasting one

Memory Work

Review your memory work.

I P. 1.6-7 So these have come so that your faith which is of greater wealth than gold, which persists when refined by fire, may prove genuine and result in praise honor + glory when Jesus is revealed

Prayer Time

Pair off in twos. Read aloud Stephen Olford's opening challenge on Day 5. Then confess to each other an area where you have neglected to allow Jesus to be Lord. Pray for each other. If someone does not want to pray audibly, she can pray silently.

Three

Precious, Chosen, and Beloved

This journey through earth *is* difficult, and just like Christ, you *will* experience suffering—*but you are God's own*. He has called you, He loves you, He sees you as precious and beloved. Just as He chose the Israelites and cared for them, provided for them, and led them in their journey across the desert to the Promised Land, so will He do that for you. He also has a purpose for your life. Have you ever felt like a second-class citizen as a woman? The world may treat you like that, but that isn't the way God sees you. Note that the memory work showing the high calling of God on your life is not gender specific—it is a call to all of God's children: male *and* female. You can be confident in God's love and calling for your life.

Memory Work
Memorize 1 Peter 2:9-10 by memorizing the song "Chosen Generation" on page 136.

Warm-Up
In 1 Peter 2:9-11, it is clear that God has called you for a purpose. He has a plan for your life. In **one** breath share just **one** purpose that seems clear to you. Be specific and personal. (For example: Amy might say: "I'm a new mother and I am called to raise Benjamin to love and serve God." Linda might say: "I'm a stylist and I am called to show my clients Christ's love and to be ready to give an answer for the hope within me.")

Day 1: Like Newborn Babes

How I remember those precious days when I was breastfeeding. A tiny little head would grope frantically until he found the nipple; then he would seize it and guzzle intently, perspiration soaking his downy head. Eventually he would slow down, satisfied and sleepy, his tiny eyelids at half-mast. It amazed me to see my baby grow big and strong on breast milk alone.

This is the metaphor Peter uses. Just as we have been born again by the word of God (1:23), we are now to be nourished by the Word of God, and to desire it as earnestly as a newborn babe desires his mother's breast.

*1. Describe, in detail, how a newborn evidences his desire for milk.

starts sucking. he cries - in distress. cranky

*Do you have that same desire for the Word of God? If so, give evidence.

2. With the same hunger of a newborn, read 1 Peter 2 as an overview. Find evidences that though this life is difficult, God loves you intensely and is caring for you. Be ready for God to show you something for today. Write it down here and explain how you will apply it.

v.5 He's building us into his spiritual household despite the influence of malice, deceit, hypocrisy, envy, slander-(v1) like a mom feeds a baby - God feeds us when we cry out. v.9 I belong to God

*Read 1 Peter 2:1-3 out loud to yourself.

3. Here Peter lists five relational sins: malice, deceit, hypocrisy, envy, and slander. The following women exemplify these sins. Explain how the sin affected the woman and/or others.

A. Malice (Herodias in Matthew 14:3-12) _desire to cause injury. John beheaded. The sin overtook the woman and distress Herod. It also affected Jesus + followers_

B. Deceit (Leah and her father in Genesis 29:16-35)

Leah was given to Jacob instead of Rachel.

C. Hypocrisy (Sapphira in Acts 5:1-11) – *lied about a financial gift*
She was struck dead

D. Envy (Miriam in Numbers 12) – *Miriam was envious of the reputation Moses had as a spokesman for God. leprosy, seven days stop of the journey*

E. Slander (Potiphar's wife in Genesis 39)
She spoke lies of Joseph

Personal Action Assignment

As you are still before God, do you see any of the these relational sins in your life? Kneel before Him and ask Him to search your heart. If you are having a problem in a horizontal relationship, it is almost always because you have a problem in your vertical relationship with God. Rid yourself of any sin through confession and repentance. Is there any person you have wronged and from whom you should ask forgiveness? If so, do.

*4. What reasons are given for craving God's Word in 1 Peter 2:2-3?
So that we may grow in our salvation

5. In verse 3, Peter is alluding to Psalm 34:8, to which he will return in chapter 3. In this psalm we are told "taste and see that the Lord is good." Give one example of how God has shown you His goodness recently.
His provision of a new home – friends in the family of God

Memory Work

Sing "Chosen Generation" several times.

Day 2: The Rock — Your Demise or Your Salvation?

When Peter sat at the feet of Jesus, he was often confused by His mysterious parables. When Jesus told the Parable of the Tenants, He said one group would come to a "wretched end," the other group would be blessed. The disciples were confused. Gently Jesus asked:

> *"Have you never read the Scriptures: 'The stone the builders rejected has become the capstone; the Lord has done this, and it is marvelous in our eyes'? . . . He who falls on this stone will be broken to pieces, but he on whom it falls will be crushed." (Matthew 21:42b, 44)*

What could the Master mean? Edmund Clowney writes:

> *Peter had learned that the death of Christ was not an unthinkable defeat for the Son of God and the kingdom of God. Rather, by the cross and the resurrection God's eternal purpose of salvation had been fulfilled. Those who had crucified Jesus had accomplished what God's power and will had decided beforehand should happen (Acts 4:28). In their rejection of Christ, the builders, in spite of themselves, served to put God's Stone in place.[17]*

As you read the prophecies that Jesus fulfilled, as you study the stirring sermon of Peter at Pentecost, stand in awe of God. Do not resist this mighty God, seek refuge in Him!

6.   What do each of the following prophecies teach you about Jesus?
     A. Isaiah 28:16

     B. Psalm 118:19-23

Read Matthew 21:33-46.
7.   The tenants represent the Jews, the servants represent the prophets, the son, Jesus. What did the tenants do to the servants? To the son?

What will the owner of the vineyard therefore do to those tenants?

Read Acts 4:1-22.

8. Describe what happened to Peter and John. What was Peter's message?

How did Peter and John respond when they were told to obey the order from the government to stop teaching in the name of Jesus?

Read 1 Peter 2:4-8.
*9. Record *everything* you can discover about those who do not believe.

*Record *everything* you can discover about those who do believe.

In verse 6, the "never be put to shame" is an especially strong negative construction, like our English "never, never" or "absolutely never."

10. You can either resist the Rock or find shelter in the Rock. What do you learn from the image given in each of the following?
    A. Exodus 33:21-23

    B. Song of Songs 2:14

In your personal quiet time, sing "Rock of Ages" (see p. 137). Find shelter in the Rock today for this day's storms.

*11. Not only can those who trust daily in Christ find shelter, but Peter gives some other promises. Find them in 1 Peter 2:5-6.

Memory Work
Sing "Chosen Generation" in praise to the Lord. Can you sing it by heart?

Day 3: You are a Chosen Generation
You belong to God, you are His precious daughter, and He has chosen you for a purpose. Again, Peter parallels our journey as Christians through earth with the journey the Children of Israel made from Egypt, through the desert, to the Promised Land. Just as God chose them, called them out of Egypt, cared for them in the desert, and loved them, even in their rebellion, so He does the same with us who have been grafted in to the branch of Israel. We too are chosen. We too are beloved and cared for by our Heavenly Father.

Read 1 Peter 2:9-10.
*12. According to this passage, describe your identity in detail (vv. 9a and 10).

chosen, royal priesthood, holy nation, belonging to God able to declare His praises - having experienced darkness + now light. People of God having received mercy

Read Isaiah 43:16-21.
13. Isaiah is painting a mural. Describe what you see (vv. 16-19).

_The Egyptians being defeated in the Red Sea.
God preparing a way in the desert
Animals honoring God because of His provision_

Are there any enemy chariots chasing you? If so, what are they?

Fear / anxiety

What will God do for you if you trust in Him? (v. 19)

take it away / provide peace + assurance of His control

14. What does Isaiah call God's people? (v. 20b)

"my people" "my chosen"

What is God's purpose for our lives? (v. 21b)

*That we proclaim His praises
make Him known!*

Find the similarities between the preceeding passage and 1 Peter 2:9-10.

*we are chosen, belonging to God - to declare His praises -
because He provided a way into His presence.*

Read Exodus 19:1-6.

15. What message from God does Moses communicate to the Israelites?

*He wants us to be His special kingdom of priests and a holy nation
Even though the whole earth is His - His people will be set apart*

How is this similar to 1 Peter 2:9?

God's people are chosen by Him to be special

16. Read Exodus 12:1–19:6 and list some of the ways God cared for, nourished, and protected His people. (You will be blessed as you realize that God is saying in 1 Peter: "Just as I cared for the Children of Israel, I am caring for you. You are My chosen people.")

Memory Work
Sing "Chosen Generation" by heart.

*Thurs. May 30 '02
8 am*

Day 4: Women, We Are Priests, and We Must Be Holy!
Recording artist Kathy Troccoli and I are doing some women's conferences together. Recently she told me, "Before I went out there, God told me, 'Kathy: you've got to be holy.'"

Beth Moore, speaker and author, mentioned the same thing. Before she was going to speak at a conference, her daughter wanted to turn on the TV in the motel room. Beth said, "No, honey—I can't have any of the world in me. I need to be holy when I go in to those women."

Just as we who are speaking and singing at Christian women's conferences need to be holy, so do we as women in general. A priest is one who presents God to the people (and the people to God). Is this not our calling as mothers, mentors, and women who are in this world? Do we not want the Spirit of God to fall upon our homes, our offices, our spirits? Then we must be pure, holy. We are a royal priesthood!

In the Old Testament, only the high priests could enter the holy of holies. Today, because of Christ, all believers are able to enter the holy place. Just as the priests needed to purify themselves before entering, so do we. We cannot expect to receive from God in our time with Him if we have unconfessed sin, evil motives, or a proud heart.

17. Moses and Aaron followed carefully the rules God laid down for a priest. Describe how God responded in Leviticus 9:23-24.

God was pleased and consumed the sacrifice. The glory of the Lord appeared to them

18. In Leviticus 10:1-3:

A. How did Aaron's sons show disrespect for God? (v. 1)

They didn't follow the law and Gods fire destroyed them

B. What happened to them? (v. 2)

they were consumed by God's fire & died

C. What reason did Moses give for their deaths? (v. 3)

God was showing Himself Holy. He could not accept the disrespectful, unholy sacrifice

D. How did Aaron show his respect for the Lord? (v. 3)

Aaron remained silent. He could have argued or question Moses + the Lord but he didit

This judgment seems harsh to us, but we must understand that God was using this generation of priests to teach all subsequent generations how to approach Almighty Yahweh. Moses' explanation was clear: those who share the privilege of being nearest to God must also bear the awesome responsibility of exemplifying His holiness through obedience. "Unto whomsoever much is given, of him shall be much required." (Luke 12:48)[18]

19. Are you a pure woman, a holy woman? Pray through Psalm 139:23-24 and record any thoughts for yourself which these verses prompt.

If you have a family, do they think of you as a pure woman? *cleanliness before God.*

Memory Work
Review 1 Peter 1:3.

Day 5: A People Belonging to God

The NIV says we are "a people belonging to God" (1 Peter 2:9). This brings images of betrothal to my mind, a picture God often uses in Scripture to show us that just as a husband and wife belong to one another and must be true to one another, so do we belong to Christ and must be faithful to Him, as His treasured wife.

20. God told the Prophet Hosea to marry an adulteress as a picture to Israel of their relationship with God. Read the following passages from Hosea and list what you learn about Israel in 2:5; 2:8; and 2:13.

5: Israel was unfaithful - chasing after other gods thinking they will provide for their people
8: Didn't acknowledge God as being their loving provider
13: Israel will be punished for her lusting after other gods

God disciplined Israel for her unfaithfulness and then He called her to Him. What do you learn about this in Hosea 2:14-23?

God truly loves his people and is not willing that they stay away from him - He wants them back. He seems to humble himself to get them back.

How is Hosea 2:23b similar to 1 Peter 2:10?

God calls them "my people" after once not being his people.

21. How does it make you feel to know you are chosen, you are holy, you are betrothed and belong to God? *Safe, loved, chosen.*
In awe, amazed,

Are you faithful to God? Is He first? Do you always spend time with Him daily? Do you run to Him first? Do you converse constantly with Him?

Memory Work
Review 1 Peter 1:7.

Wed June 5 9am

Day 6: A Stranger on Earth

Peter tells us we are strangers on earth, just passing through. We must hold this world loosely or it will be a snare to us. God gives us good gifts to thankfully enjoy, but if we set our hearts on them they will lure us off the path of true joy and into destruction.

22. Read Luke 17:26-33.

A. Describe the spiritual insensitivity of people in the days of Noah. What happened to them? *They went about life conquer and with a notion that God + his righteousness intervene in their day*

B. Describe the spiritual insensitivity of people in the days of Lot and what happened to them.

> same

indifferent

C. God promised to rescue Lot and his family from judgment. What did Lot's wife do? (Need help? See Genesis 19:15-26.) Why was this wrong and what did it show about her attitude toward life? *God provided a way out for them. They bargained for another place (town) and even then Lot's wife was unaware of God's power for she looked back - lack of trust. Clinging to world*

D. What warning does Jesus give in Luke 17:33? *Do not try to hold on to this life because we will only lose it!*

In *Pilgrim's Progress* Christian and Hopeful are tempted on their journey by Money-Love and Demas, who ask them to leave the path and come to the silver mine to get rich. Hopeful says, "Let's go and see."[19] But Christian resists, reminding Hopeful of how the desire to get rich can be a snare. As they travel a little further they come upon a monument of salt in the form of a woman. On it was written: "Remember Lot's wife."

What we let go God will save.

Hopeful says: "I marvel that I have not been punished as she was.
Our sins are the same. She only looked back; I wanted to go to the silver pit.
Thank God for his grace and let me be ashamed of my desires."[20]

We belong to a different country. This world is not our home, and we must not cling to it. The KJV translates "a people belonging to God" in 1 Peter 2:9 as "a peculiar people." We have a different Master, belong to a different country, and have a different purpose than the people of this world.

*22. How does Peter describe us in verse 11a?

aliens, strangers

*Often we choose sin because we think it is the easy way out (lying, abortion, sloth. . .). What is the truth? (v. 11b) *These temptations war @ our soul when we give in we are losing another battle. Satan gains more foothold*

How can you apply this today? *Robbing us of peace, confidence and joy by giving us dissatisfaction w/ ourselves.*

*How does Peter tell us to live and why? (v. 12) *Our lives should be full of good deeds that point to God. they may accuse us now, but they will see the truth when He returns!*

23. It is hard to travel through this world and not adopt its customs. The Children of Israel often failed in this. Read each of the following rebukes from the prophets and describe how Israel had become like the world. What personal warning do you see in each?

    A. Isaiah 1:1-17

    B. Isaiah 2:6-8

    C. Isaiah 3:16-24

    D. Malachi 2:13-16

    E. Malachi 3:6-12

24. As you consider the customs of your world, the ways people spend their time, their money, their thoughts—the way they relate to one another—are there any customs you have picked up that take you away from or reflect poorly on Jesus, your First Love?

*materialism
eating out at super expense*

25. What do you think you will remember from this week's study?

Memory Work

Sing "Chosen Generation."

Prayer Time

In circles of three or four, lift up your own request in prayer. Then one or two can support you with a sentence. When there is a pause, another person lifts up her own request. For example:

Annie: Please help me to establish the habit of a quiet time.
Sally: Please help Annie get out of bed in the morning, hungry for You.
Beth: I agree, Lord.
Pause

Four

Understanding Submission
in the Context of 1 Peter

 utside football stadiums filled with Promise Keepers marched women with placards from NOW, the feminist National Organization for Women.

Promise Keepers Unfair to Women!
Equality for Women!

Though these protesters had not heard the whole message, they were deeply offended by the soundbites they *had* heard: "The man is the head of the home" and "Be the spiritual leader in your home."

How important that those seeking the truth hear the whole message. The passage we are approaching, 1 Peter 3:1-7, is a prime example. Many women have been told they cannot speak to their unbelieving husbands, they cannot wear any jewelry (even wedding rings), and they must obey their husbands in all things, even if the demand is to submit to an abortion. All of this is false, a distortion that comes from ripping verses out of context. The reader who doesn't take the time to see the whole picture may misinterpret the soundbites.

Because this passage is directed to us as women, we are going to spend three weeks on it, getting off the train as we often do in this *Woman's Journey* series when a scene is of particular relevance to us. Before we examine the details closely next week, we must understand the overview. We don't want to be like NOW, who, though they may be well-intentioned, missed the forest for the trees.

The whole context of 1 Peter deals with submission, not just for wives, but for everyone. And who is our model? Jesus.

Come, explore the *whole* truth.

Memory Work

Memorize 1 Peter 2:23. Extra credit? Do the whole passage below.

> [21]To this you were called, because Christ suffered for you, leaving you an example, that you should follow in his steps. [22]"He committed no sin, and no deceit was found in his mouth." **[23]When they hurled their insults at him, he did not retaliate; when he suffered, he made no threats. Instead, he entrusted himself to him who judges justly.** [24]He himself bore our sins in his body on the tree, so that we might die to sins and live for righteousness; by his wounds you have been healed. [25]For you were like sheep going astray, but now you have returned to the Shepherd and Overseer of your souls. (1 Peter 2:21-25)

Warm-Up

Call out some painful or embarrassing mistakes that occurred because you failed to slow down and look at context. (You brushed your teeth with diaper ointment, hugged a man you thought was your husband from behind, put a cup of salt in the cake. . . .)

Day 1: Submit Yourself to Every Authority

In a few days we will look at Peter's admonition to women who are married to men who do not obey the Word: "*Wives, in the same way be submissive.*" What does Peter mean by "*in the same way*"? James Slaughter explains:

> "In the same way" refers to the more all-encompassing exhortation to submit for the Lord's sake to others in various relationships instituted among human beings . . . . He spoke to mistreated slaves (2:18-21), to harried wives (3:1-6) and hassled husbands (3:7), to believers struggling in civil affairs (3:8-4:19), to church elders threatened by younger people (5:1-4), and to younger people in the church chafing under the leadership of an older generation (5:5). In all those relationships they were to carry out the exhortation of 2:13-17. . . . **The behavior of believers when they encounter unfair circumstances should reflect a spirit of deference in all relationships as they follow Christ's example and anticipate future glory.**[21]

Read 1 Peter 2:13-3:7 as an overview.

1. List all the persons who are told to submit, to whom, and why. Give verse references.

Read 1 Peter 2:13-17.
*2. Who is told to submit here, to whom, and for whose sake? (v. 13)

What do you think Peter means by "for the Lord's sake"?

> *Of course, everything, we do should be for the glory of God and the good of His kingdom! But Peter was careful to point out the Christians in society are representatives of Jesus Christ.—Warren Wiersbe[22]*

3. Why should you obey laws about speeding, littering, etc.? Do you?

*4. What will silence the ignorant talk of foolish men? (v. 15)

"Doing good" is a powerful tool, whether you are dealing with an unfair government, boss, husband, or mother-in-law. If possible, share a time when you (or someone else) were treated unfairly, responded with love, and saw God's power displayed.

Did this increase your confidence in God? Explain.

5. Some of the early Christians felt their freedom in Christ freed them from the law. What does Peter say in verse 16?

In Romans 12:17-13:5, what thoughts parallel 1 Peter 2:13-17?

*6.   In 1 Peter 2:18-20 who is told to submit, to whom, and why?

To what two kinds of masters are they to submit?

Slavery was an unjust institution. The rise of Christianity has often meant its demise. I would encourage you to rent the movie *Amistad*. There is a wonderful historical scene where the slaves look at the pictures of Jesus, the suffering servant, and come to faith in him. I would also encourage you to read the classic, *Uncle Tom's Cabin*, by Harriet Beecher Stowe, which has often been cited as starting the Civil War and overturning slavery in America. In the story, the slaveowners, often because of the witness of Christian slaves, began to struggle with their consciences. The following account occurs between Tom and his owner, Cassy:

> "Missis," said Tom, after a while, "I can see that, somehow, you're quite 'bove me in everything; but there's one thing Missis might learn even from poor Tom. . . .The Lord hasn't forgot us,—I'm sartin' o' that ar'. If we suffer with him, we shall also reign, Scripture says. . . ."
> Cassy took the book . . . . She then read aloud. . .often, as she read, her voice faltered. . . . When she came to the touching words, "Father forgive them, for they know not what they do," she threw down the book, and burying her face in the heavy masses of her hair, she sobbed aloud, with a convulsive violence.[23]

7. Read the following accounts of the apostles taking unjust punishment for the sake of Christ. How do you think this impacted witnesses?
     A. Acts 5:40-42

B. Acts 16:22-25

When Christian men and women took cruel sufferings patiently and joyfully, as the apostles did . . . it showed the power of Christian motives.[24]

Memory Work

Write out 1 Peter 2:23 and put it on your mirror to start work on it.

Day 2: Entrusting Ourselves to the One Who Judges Justly

Corrie ten Boom tells of hiding a little Bible under her dress as she walked past the guards in the concentration camp:

It made a bulge you could have seen across the Grote Markt. I flattened it out as best I could . . . but there was no real concealing it beneath the thin cotton dress. And all the while I had the incredible feeling that it didn't matter, that this was not my business, but God's. That all I had to do was walk straight ahead.

As we trooped back out through the shower room door, the S.S. men ran their hands over every prisoner, front, back, and sides. The woman ahead of me was searched three times. Behind me, Betsie was searched. No hand touched me.[25]

As you travel through this world, you will experience pain. As you seek to serve God, you will experience spiritual warfare. Peter reminds us: *If you do what is right, and if you follow in the steps of Christ and commit yourself to the One who judges justly, God will be your Advocate.* How that wonderful truth leads to confidence.

Read 1 Peter 2:21-25.
*9. How does Peter begin verse 21?

*10. Find all the reasons Christ suffered (vv. 21, 24).

*11. Describe how Christ suffered. Find His secret (vv. 22-23).

We need not be concerned about maintaining our rights. Jesus trusted his Father, the righteous Judge, to do that; and so should we. . . . This is the life of Christian pilgrims in this world.[26]

How does Paul tell us to handle unjust treatment in Romans 12:19?

Is there a situation in your life right now where you are being treated unfairly? Commit your case to God. He cares and He is a God of justice.

Peter is quoting from Isaiah, who predicted Christ's sufferings seven hundred years before they happened. He also predicted Christ would respond with quiet confidence. (Isaiah 53)

12. Isaiah and Peter tell us we are like sheep who have gone astray. Now we have returned to the shepherd and overseer of our souls. List three specific differences that is making in your life.

Sing: "Surely Goodness and Mercy" (p. 138).

The pilgrims cross the river of death to the Celestial City. "After the suffering of his soul, he will see the light of life, and be satisfied." (Isaiah 53:11)

Memory Work
Memorize 1 Peter 2:23.

Day 3: Wives, in the Same Way

Are you beginning to see why the context of this passage is so crucial? The primary purpose of Peter's whole letter was to help believers of all kinds prepare to suffer for Christ—the fiery trials and persecutions had begun, and they were going to intensify. Believers in general would be persecuted, Christian slaves would be treated harshly, and women who came to faith apart from their husbands could expect an angry reaction. James Slaughter explains: "Relating to others in a godly way always presents a challenge, but this is especially so when people are treated unjustly. This was the case with Peter's audience."[27] Slaughter writes:

> Here Peter addressed the severest relationship for a wife, namely, marriage to an unbelieving husband. A wife is to submit to her husband even if he is "disobedient to the word." Vaughn and Lea comment that "disobedient" (in the Greek) is a strong word, implying open and active hostility to the gospel.[28]

*13. Read 1 Peter 3:1-7 as an overview.

Today, make as many observations as you can concerning the first four verses. See if you can come up with *at least* five for each verse, though ten would be better. (They are there—you just have to keep looking! Howard Hendricks, a teacher of Bible study methods for many years, had a reputation for making his students find ten observations from a single verse. They would come back proudly and he'd say: "Do it again!" This would go on for days—even weeks.) Note comparisons, warnings, word pictures. Explore cross-references and different translations. Ask questions—don't worry if you don't have the answer, it will provoke thinking—and that's how a good detective gets to the truth. You will be amazed at how much you discover simply by making observations. I've gotten you started on verse 1.

3:1
This is addressed to wives of husbands who do not obey the Word.
It says "in the same way" so a comparison is being made.
Is that comparison to Jesus? Is it to slaves? Is Peter saying wives are slaves?

3:2

3:3

3:4

14. What stood out to you from this exercise?

Day 4: Husbands, in the Same Way

Again, we see a pattern in Peter—it isn't just women who are told to submit, but all believers. A man is not to take advantage of his position as head of the home. Peter has some severe warnings for the husband who does that.

*15. Continue your observations of 1 Peter 3:1-7, beginning with verse 5.
Find at least five, but try for ten for each verse. Remember not to be afraid to ask questions. Pray that God will show you the answers as the study continues.

3:5

3:6

3:7

*16. What stood out to you from the above exercise and why?

Memory Work
Memorize 1 Peter 2:23.

Day 5: The Importance of Context

One of the devices of false teachers is to take Scripture out of context. For example, the Book of Ecclesiastes was written, in part, to show the futility of living a life apart from God. Many of the statements made are from the desperate lips of a person who is trying to find meaning apart from God—but he cannot. He continually cries throughout the book:

"Meaningless! Meaningless!"
says the Teacher.
"Utterly meaningless!
Everything is meaningless." (Ecclesiastes 1:2)

Taken out of context, you might include that God's Word says there is no meaning in life. However, that would be false, for God's Word is clear that when you know Christ there is great meaning in life! Haven't you read again and again in 1 Peter that you have been called for a purpose?

One of the reasons I've encouraged you to ask questions when you are observing a passage of Scripture is to cause you to look at the context of all of Scripture. Perhaps you have come up with some interesting questions through your observations of 1 Peter 3:1-7. I hope so, for it is a passage that is often misinterpreted—and you need to find the truth. From the first verse alone you might have asked:

Is Peter saying wives are the same as slaves?

Is Peter saying that if a woman is married to an unbeliever that she can't talk to him about Jesus?

If you take verse 1 out of context, you might answer yes to both of the above questions. However, placed in the context of all of Scripture, the answer is no to both of the above.

17. When Peter says, "in the same way," he is referring back to the model of Jesus and His unjust treatment, and to slaves and their unjust treatment, but the whole context moves all the way back to 1 Peter 2:13. What does that say?

The opening words [of 1 Peter 3:1-6] are not intended to equate the submissiveness due from wives with that expected from slaves. Rather, as in [verse] 7, the Greek adverb harks back to 2:13, implying that the patriarchal principle of the subordination of the wife to her husband is not a matter of human convention but the order which the Creator has established.[29]

18. When you come up with a question, it is good to try to answer it by looking not only at the verse that provoked the question, but also at other Scriptures on

the same topic. For example, we know that other Scriptures refute the equation of wives to slaves. What do you learn concerning this from each of the following?

    A. 1 Peter 3:7b

    B. Genesis 1:26-27

    C. Ephesians 5:25-33

Since wives are not slaves, then why is there a comparison? It is because if they were married to men who did not obey the Word, they might experience the same kind of harsh treatment that a slave might experience from a harsh master—and they, like slaves, and like Jesus, needed to entrust themselves to Him who judges justly (see 1 Peter 2:23b). One beneficial result is that this is the most effective way to win an unbeliever to the Lord. This leads to our next question: Are wives not to talk about Jesus to their unbelieving husbands?

Memory Work
Review 1 Peter 2:23. Extra time? Begin memorizing the context: 1 Peter 2:21-25. It is a wonderful passage which you will use!

Day 6: Winning without Words
One of my favorite quotations is from Saint Francis of Assisi (1182–1226):

Preach the gospel all the time ... and if necessary use words.

In many ways that sums up what Peter is saying. It isn't that wives married to unbelieving husbands could not speak, it is that they had to be cautious—for nagging and arguments would not win their husbands.

19. If you keep reading in 1 Peter 3, how can you see from verse 15 that a wife may have to use words in order to win her husband to Christ?

Describe, on the basis of 1 Peter 3:15, how she should speak those words.

20. What do you learn about how she should not use words according to the following passages?
 A. Proverbs 19:13b

 B. Proverbs 21:9, 19

 C. Proverbs 27:15-16

 D. 2 Timothy 2:25-26

A tangent to interpreting Scripture in context is not to press the details when a parable or word picture is given, but to look for the main point. For example, when Psalm 91 talks about finding refuge in the wings of God, it does not mean God has wings! In 1 Peter 3:1 you will find what grammarians refer to as antanaclasis, commonly known as a pun.[30] A pun, like a parable, paints a memorable picture, but you need to take the whole idea and not press each detail. Here it is in a translation and a paraphrase, with the pun in bold.

> NIV: "If any of them do not believe **the word**, they may be won over without **words** by the behavior of their wives, when they see the purity and reverence of your lives."

> J.B. Phillips: "If they do not obey the **Word** of God they may be won to God without any **word** being spoken, simply by seeing the pure and reverent behavior of you, their wives."

21. What is the main point of 1 Peter 3:1?

Why might pressing all the details in a parable, word picture, or pun lead to misinterpretation? What might happen, for example, if you did that with 1 Peter 3:1?

22. What stood out to you from this week?

Memory Work
Review your memory verses from the first four weeks (p. 133).

Prayer Time
One effective way to pray is to pray through Scripture. Pair off and pray through 1 Peter 3:4 for one another. For example:

> *Julie: Father, please be with Karen as she raises her toddlers. When they are disobedient, help Karen to be firm but gentle—to have that calm and gentle spirit which is so precious in Your sight.*
> *Karen: I agree, Lord. I would ask the same for Julie—especially as she raises her strong-willed daughter. May we so radiate Your gentleness and love that our children will be drawn to You.*

Five

Winsome, Winning Women

A perfume commercial seductively asks: "What is she wearing?" Singer and author Kathy Troccoli answers:

Jesus. The answer must be Jesus . . . Jesus is my beauty. He is my loveliness, my confidence, my charisma.[31]

Have you ever met someone whom you suspected was a Christian because of the beauty and quiet confidence that flowed from her spirit? Kathy tells of meeting a flight attendant like that:

An undeniable radiance exuded from her person. I was sure she was a Christian— the way she smiled, the way she showed patience, kindness, and grace to everyone she encountered. . . . While I'd never done anything like this before, somehow I had to ask her. . . I even surprised myself as I asked, "You love Jesus, don't you?"

She looked up at me, and with a glow in her eyes, she said, "Yes, how did you know?" I told her I had watched her and that her actions and her countenance spoke loudly to me about her love for him. The river of life inside of that flight attendant splashed onto everyone around her. And if she had never spoken a word that day, all those coming in contact with her would have seen clearly the God of the universe living inside of her heart.[32]

That's what Peter is talking about in this passage. When the river of life is flowing inside us, unhindered by sin, we are beautiful women. Without even speaking a word, people are drawn to the One who is consecrated in our hearts.

Memory Work

Memorize 1 Peter 3:4. Extra credit? Do the whole passage below.

> *¹Wives, in the same way be submissive to your husbands so that, if any of them do not believe the word, they may be won over without words by the behavior of their wives, ²when they see the purity and reverence of your lives. ³Your beauty should not come from outward adornment, such as braided hair and the wearing of gold jewelry and fine clothes.* **⁴Instead, it should be that of your inner self, the unfading beauty of a gentle and quiet spirit, which is of great worth in God's sight.** *(1 Peter 3:1-4)*

Warm-Up

Have you ever suspected that someone loved Jesus because of her countenance and behavior? If so, what did you particularly notice? (Hear from a few.)

Day 1: It Wasn't Easy Being a Woman

Women were treated poorly before Christianity. They were not seen as equals, but as property. Remember how shocked the disciples were when they found Jesus teaching the Samaritan woman? Or how ruffled Martha was that her sister Mary was sitting at Jesus' feet instead of helping her in the kitchen? Jesus was a revolutionary: He shocked the world then and He is still in the business of changing prejudiced hearts today. I so appreciate men like John Dawson, founder of International Reconciliation Coalition, who humbly confessed in a foreword to the book *Women of Destiny:*

> *I am part of a patriarchal religious culture in which women who serve ministries are usually treated with great kindness but seldom taken seriously as leaders.*[33]

I believe the Spirit of God is doing a new work in allowing women in the church to be treated seriously. However, we *have* come a long way because of Jesus. I have a young friend who is committing her life to helping oppressed women in countries where the influence of Christianity has been minimal—the stories she tells make me so thankful for the light of Christ. If you lived in those countries, or if you lived in Peter's day, you would realize how much Christ has freed women. It is important to understand this setting in which Peter writes.

B.C. Caffin explains:

> Christianity was in its infancy; it was to be the means of abolishing slavery, and of raising woman to her proper place in society; but as yet slaves were cruelly oppressed, and women were ill treated and despised. . . . Christianity would introduce a great and sweeping change in the relations of the sexes, as well as in the relations of master and slave. But the change must be gradual, not violent; it must be brought about by the softening and purifying influences of religion, not by revolt against recognized customs and established authority.[34]

1. In each of the following find evidence that the attitude toward women in biblical times was in great need of enlightenment. Find examples of unbelievers, believers, men, and women holding women in low esteem.
  *A. Genesis 19:1-8

  B. Judges 19

  C. Ruth 2:5

  D. 1 Kings 11:3

  E. Esther 1:10–2:4

*F. Malachi 2:13-16

*G. Luke 24:9-11

In the last example Luke, who was a physician, used a Greek word (translated "nonsense") which means "the delirious talk of the very ill!"

2. Find evidence that Christ's attitude toward women was revolutionary:
    *A. John 4:27

    B. Luke 10:38-42

    *C. John 20:10-18

Because women were seen as property, as inferior, as servants rather than coheirs, a wife was expected to adopt the religion of her husband. Plutarch reflects these sentiments:

> *A wife ought not to make friends on her own, but to enjoy her husband's friends in common with him. The gods are the first and most important friends. . . .*[35]

When a wife refused to worship her husband's gods because she had come to know Christ, James Slaughter explains that "she became vulnerable to sharp criticism and harsh treatment from him."[36] She also became suspect of the state for, as Edmund Clowney explains:

> This became an issue in Roman history when many women were attracted to the cult of Bacchus. . . . The rituals of Bacchus had been banned by the Roman Senate. . . . In the eyes of imperial Romans, here was another subversive Eastern religion threatening the stability of the home and of the state.[37]

3. How does understanding the culture of the day help you to understand Peter's counsel to women in 1 Peter 3:1-2?

4. Why do you think Peter says "to your own husbands"?

The above point is crucial, showing that Peter was not saying that all women are under the authority of all men. This was revolutionary, reflecting the light of Christ.

> [The Greek phrase translated "to your own" is used] to clarify and limit a wife's responsibility to submit. Peter underscored his focus on subordination within marriage, not outside it. As Beare remarks, [the Greek phrase] is perhaps needed to prevent ambiguity, to make clear that it is subjection in the marital relationship, not a general subjection of women to men that is required.[38]

Memory Work
Begin memorizing 1 Peter 3:4.

Day 2: Unequally Yoked
In her book, *Beloved Unbeliever*, Jo Berry gives a word picture of what the Bible calls being "unequally yoked" (a partnership, whether it is a marriage or a business partnership between a believer and an unbeliever).

> One of the favorite events at the Little League picnic was a father/son three-legged race. . . . It was amusing for those fathers and sons to be linked together in that race, as mismatched as they were in size . . . we laughed so hard we got tears in

our eyes. . . . But I noticed that the first thing each father and son did, when they either dropped out or crossed the finish line, was untie the cords that were binding them together. . . . I wonder how many of them would have considered staying tied together for the rest of their lives? . . . Doesn't sound like much fun, does it?[39]

In *Pilgrim's Progress*, the husband comes to faith first. However, after he crosses the river of death, doubts assail his wife. The Holy Spirit awakens her from her apathy. One day she is mulling over her thoughts when a messenger named Secret appears:

Peace be to this House! . . . I dwell in the city where Christian has gone. It is thought by the people where I live that you desire to go there. It is reported that you are sorry for the way you treated your husband in setting yourself against his good life, and in keeping your children in ignorance of the way everlasting.[40]

After Secret leaves, Christiana calls her children to her and tells them of the guilt she feels for the great sin of not going with their father.

"Then she said to her children, 'Sons, we are all undone.'"

5.   What reasons are given in 2 Corinthians 6:14-18 for not entering into an unequal yoke?

The wives Peter was addressing had probably not entered into an unequal yoke, but instead had converted after they were married. But whether a marriage is an unequal yoke because of disobedience, ignorance, or conversion after marriage, the advice Peter gives applies. There is hope, if you are in such a situation, that you can win your husband to Christ through your behavior.

Read 1 Corinthians 7:12-18.
*6.   What counsel is given here to the wife in an unequal yoke? (v. 13)

*Why? (v. 14)

Sanctified means "set apart." The unbelieving spouse is "set apart" by God for special treatment. God is wooing him that the marriage might be a Christian unity.

7.   Sometimes the unbelieving partner will come to Christ—other times, he or she wants to leave. According to 1 Corinthians 7:15, what should the wife in an unequal yoke do if the husband wants to leave?

What hope does Paul give the spouse in an unequal yoke? (v. 16)

8.   To what three institutions among men has Peter thus far referred? (2:13; 2:18; 3:1)

Slavery was an evil institution that did not have God's blessing. However, God ordained both government and marriage. "Marriage should be honored by all,"

Hebrews 13:4a tells us. Just as God can move in the hearts of unbelieving kings, He can move in the hearts of unbelieving husbands to accomplish His goals. In *Beloved Unbeliever*, Jo Berry tells of a young wife who never sought her husband's counsel because he was an unbeliever, but became convicted by the Word that she was wrong.

> *Susie learned that she dare not shut out her husband from any facet of her life. The unequally yoked wife must respect her spouse's position as God's representative authority, trusting that He will work through her husband to accomplish His will in her life and marriage.[41]*

Personal Action Assignment

Spend some time in prayer for the women you know who are in an unequal yoke. Pray 1 Peter 3:1-4 and 2 Timothy 2:24-26 for them.

Memory Work

Keep memorizing 1 Peter 3:4.

Day 3: 1 Peter 3 Wives

This passage is referred to so frequently to counsel women married to unbelievers that these wives have come to be known as 1 Peter 3 wives. My dear friend Lee Petno was such a wife. She took Peter's admonition very literally and did not say a word about coming to know Christ, though she did mention she'd been attending a Bible study I was leading. The first time I met her husband, Vince, he asked me: "Are you the one who is responsible for the dramatic change in my wife?" (Lee had really been practicing her gentle and quiet spirit!) I smiled and said, "No—Jesus is the One who has changed Lee." A few months later Vince put his trust in Christ.

Augustine's mother, Monnica, was a 1 Peter 3 wife. In his journal to the Lord, Augustine wrote:

> *She served her husband as her master, and did all she could to win him for You, speaking to him of You by her conduct, by which You made her beautiful. . . . Finally, when her husband was at the end of his earthly span, she gained him for You.[42]*

There is no guarantee, but a strong possibility. I have another dear friend who has been living out the instructions in 1 Peter 3 for nearly twenty years and, outwardly, we see no change in her husband. However, there has been a tremendous change in her—she is one of the most Christlike women I know. Her daughters have seen God's love and power in her and now radiate that same love and power. When I weep for her situation she tells me how God has refined her through this marriage, teaching her to trust Him. She (and her daughters) exude a quiet confidence. Their faith is as genuine as pure gold.

9. Review what Peter says about trials in 1 Peter 1:7.

How could being married to an unbeliever help you to grow spiritually?

When Christian was journeying on earth, he reached the House Beautiful. There Charity asked him if his behavior nullified his testimony to his wife and children. He answered: "Well, indeed I cannot commend my life, for I am conscious of many failings; and I realize a person by his daily living may annul his good arguments and persuasion. Yet I was very careful not to give my family any occasion for offense at my unseemly conduct. I did not want them to be averse to going with me. But they often told me that I was too precise, that I denied myself of things in which they could see no evil."[43]

*10. Describe winning behavior according to 1 Peter 3:2.

*11. The *Word Biblical Commentary* clarifies that "reverent" refers to the wife's attitude toward God. How do you see this pattern in the following?
    1 Peter 1:17

    1 Peter 2:17-18

*12. In contrast, she is not to be frightened by her husband. How do you see this in 1 Peter 3:6b?

*How is this phrase repeated in 1 Peter 3:14?

*13. The above is extremely important, for women are not to submit because they fear their husband's reaction, but because they fear God. If they fear their husband's reaction, they might submit to sin, which we are never to do. Give some examples of how a woman who fears her husband but not God might cooperate with sin.

14. How did the Hebrew midwives demonstrate reverence toward God in Exodus 1:15-21?

How did God bless the midwives because of their reverent and pure behavior?

How is this an example of 1 Peter 2:23b?

15. How would you define purity or chastity? (1 Peter 3:2)

If you are defining purity as not sleeping with your unbelieving husband, read 1 Corinthians 7:2-5! Your marriage bed is honorable, even if your husband is an unbeliever, and you are to love him in this way as well.

Memory Work
Complete your memorization of 1 Peter 3:4.

Day 4: God's Intention for Marriage

My friend Pam often makes me laugh, like the time she said: "I had two big surprises when I became a Christian. One was that Jesus was coming back. The other was that I was to submit to my husband!"

The world definitely doesn't understand this topic, but I have found many Christian women have failed to grasp it as well. Before we can understand submission, we must understand God's purpose for marriage.

Read Genesis 2:18-25.

16. Over and over, God said during Creation, "It was good." Now something is not good. What? (v. 18a)

How does God plan to remedy the problem? (v. 18b)

17. Right after He said He will make a helper suitable for man, He does something else! What does He do? (vv. 19-20)

Why do you think God does this?

In *A Woman's Heart: God's Dwelling Place*, Beth Moore says:

> *God's task was to have Adam confront his need . . . as He gathered all those animals before Adam. That would be the first time that Adam would realize: "I'm alone here. I look across all these creatures and there is not one like me." . . . He was alone. And you see, that's God's way. He will confront us with our need and then He will appear to show us that He is the answer to that need and that He has the answer to that need.*[44]

18. A wife is called a helper. Who is also called a helper in Deuteronomy 33:29?

In Psalm 10:14?

In Psalm 27:9?

Do you think helper implies inferiority? Why or why not?

19. When God does make woman and brings her to Adam, what is Adam's response? (v. 23)

In ecstasy, man bursts into poetry upon meeting his perfect helpmeet.[45]

20. Why do you think Adam was so excited? List all the reasons you can.

21. What are some ways a woman could be truly helpful in a marriage when it comes to making decisions?

How might she be unhelpful?

22. Find and summarize God's central teaching concerning marriage from the following passages: Genesis 2:24; Matthew 19:5; and Ephesians 5:21. What is it?

23. Oneness facilitates God's three main purposes for marriage. What are those purposes according to the following Scriptures?
A. Genesis 2:18

B. Malachi 2:13-15

C. Ephesians 5:31-32

24. God longs for a husband and wife to be emotionally, sexually, and spiritually one. If you are a wife, insofar as it depends on you, what could you do to increase your harmony and intimacy with your husband:
    Emotionally?

    Sexually?

    Spiritually?

Memory Work
Review 1 Peter 1:3 and 1 Peter 1:7.

Day 5: What Is Submission?

When we realize the overwhelming teaching concerning marriage in Scripture is not, "**Who's in charge here?**" but, "**The two shall be one**," submission takes on a whole different light. J.B. Phillips helped me to receive this truth when I was a young wife through his paraphrase of Colossians 3:18:

> Wives, adapt yourselves to your husbands, that your marriage may be a Christian unity.

When a marriage is harmonious, it is able to accomplish its three central purposes (1) intimacy, (2) raising godly children, and (3) reflecting the relationship of Christ and His bride, the church.

Submit comes from the Greek word hupotasso which means "to put under" or "to subordinate." It is a voluntary act. Our word submit catches that voluntary connotation as when used in the phrase "submit an idea." I often will "submit" my thoughts to my husband. Most of the time God will cause us to be likeminded—but if not, I willingly accept his authority that our marriage might be a Christian unity.

The idea that submission means a wife is to be a doormat is erroneous. A husband needs his wife's ideas, prayers, and even gentle confrontation at times—for it was God's plan that she be his helpmate. However, if they cannot agree, then she is to willingly go under his authority. There is one exception. She is never to submit to sin.

25. Read Ephesians 5:21-33 carefully.

    A. Verse 21 sets the tone for the whole passage. Who is to submit and why?

    B. In marriage, to whom has God given the headship?

    C. How is that headship described in verses 25–30?

    D. What is the purpose of the servant authority of the husband and the respectful submission of the wife according to verse 31?

E. In a mysterious way, what does the relationship of a Christian husband and wife reflect? (v. 32)

F. How is this passage summarized in verse 33?

Even in a marriage in which the husband is an unbeliever, the wife is to submit, unless it involves sin. Just as God can work in the hearts of pagan rulers, He can work in the hearts of pagan husbands. God instituted the government, and God instituted marriage.

Memory Work
Review 1 Peter 3:4.

Day 6: The Power of Submission
The woman who kicks against the commandment to respect and to submit to her husband is missing so much. Not only is she like the foolish woman of Proverbs 14:1b who tears down her house with her own hands, but she is missing the joy, peace, and confidence that comes from a marriage that is "a Christian unity." You may be thinking: "That's fine for you, Dee—you have a godly husband. But my husband is far from the Lord. How can you expect me to submit to him?" And yet, that is exactly what Peter is asking. Things begin to happen in the heart of a man who has a submissive wife that soften him toward God.

First, a prideful and adversarial attitude builds walls, but a humble and submissive spirit breaks them down, making you and your husband closer.

26. When you have an opposing viewpoint from others, what kind of attitude on their part is most apt to make you listen to them with hearing ears? What kind of attitude is apt to make you close your heart?

Second, God is real. He blesses obedience.

27. How does God respond to a gentle and quiet spirit in each of the following passages?

1 Peter 3:9

1 Peter 3:11-12

1 Peter 3:15-16

Finally, the woman who radiates peace because of her trust in God will cause her husband to consider the reality of God. Wellington Boone, the fiery black preacher whom God has used greatly at Promise Keepers, explains that when he realized the confidence he saw in Kathryn, his future wife, was because of Jesus, he was drawn. Wellington said: "She wouldn't kiss me because I wasn't saved. That boldness put inside me a dedication to know Christ."

28. What does Peter tell us not to do in verses 6b and 14b of chapter 3?

First Peter 3:14 is a quote from Isaiah 8:12. What does Isaiah 8:12-14 say?

What are some things that people in the world fear that we do not need to fear because the Lord is our sanctuary?

Memory Work
Review 1 Peter 2:9-10 by singing "Chosen Generation" (p. 136).

Prayer Time
In circles of three or four, lift up your own request in prayer. Then one or two can support you with a sentence. When there is a pause, another person lifts up her own request.

Six

The Hidden Person of the Heart

In the same way, you wives, be submissive to your own husbands so that even if any of them are disobedient to the word they may be won without a word by the behavior of their wives, as they observe your chaste and respectful behavior, and let not your adornment be external only—braiding the hair, and wearing gold jewelry, and putting on dresses; but let it be the hidden person of the heart, with the imperishable quality of a gentle and quiet spirit, which is precious in the sight of God. For in this way in former times the holy women also, who hoped in God, used to adorn themselves, being submissive to their own husbands. Thus Sarah obeyed Abraham, calling him lord, and you have become her children if you do what is right without being frightened by any fear. (1 Peter 3:1-6)

How I love the phrase, "hidden person of the heart," which Peter uses to contrast the lasting inner beauty to our fading outer beauty. Ironically, every male commentator I've read is quick to stress that Peter isn't saying we should let ourselves go. They make me laugh—so great is their concern! Perhaps they have that reaction because they know, as males, the way Satan tries to destroy marriages by tempting them with lovely young things. But though that may be true, that is not the emphasis of this passage. Perhaps you have to be a woman to understand the enormous pressure that is *already* put on us to never grow old but to have skin that never wrinkles, hair that never grays, and a figure that never becomes matronly.

What we need *so badly* to hear as women in a world obsessed with outer appearance is the *preciousness* of the "hidden person of the heart," which, when centered on Christ, has the imperishable beauty of a gentle and quiet spirit. It is impossible to live in this world and not compare our outward beauty with that of the gorgeous young women who are constantly flashed before our eyes through the mass media. But if our confidence is in our outer person, it will erode with the years. We need to hear Peter's message with hearing ears, as badly as one lost in the desert needs an oasis. We aren't going to zip by—we are stopping for a long, cool, drink.

Memory Work
Review 1 Peter 3:4 and go on to verses 5-6.

> [4]*Instead, it should be that of your inner self, the unfading beauty of a gentle and quiet spirit, which is of great worth in God's sight.* **[5]For this is the way the holy women of the past who put their hope in God used to make themselves beautiful. They were submissive to their own husbands, [6]like Sarah, who obeyed Abraham and called him her master. You are her daughters if you do what is right and do not give way to fear.**

Warm-Up
The key phrase for inner beauty is "put their hope in God." That is the secret of confidence. It helps us choose purity when temptation is strong; it helps us be gentle and assured when maligned; and it helps us to be submissive when we wonder if our husband is making the wisest choice. Think of a time in the last year when you "put your hope in God" and He was there for you. Prepare to share it here in **one sentence.** (Hear from a few or cluster in threes and allow everyone to share.)

Day 1: The Spice Girls or the Nice Girls?
The wealthy women of Rome had memorable hairstyles.

A bust of Julia, daughter of Titus, who lived in the time of Peter[46]

J. Balsdon, in *Roman Women, Their History and Habits*, writes:

> *Curl climbs on top of curl and over the forehead there arose something which at its best looked like the chef d'oeuvre of a master pastry cook and, at its worst, like a dry sponge. At the back the hair was plaited, and the braids arranged in a coil which looks like basketwork.*[47]

Clement of Alexandria reports that women sometimes feared going to sleep at night out of concern for spoiling the design of their hair.[48] Patricia Gundry said that the wealthy woman had a full-time servant just to care for her hair![49] Correspondingly, much time and money was spent in the selection of jewelry and clothing. And while our hairstyles and fashions have changed, women today are not any less obsessed, and that monster begins when we are very young and is fed heartily throughout our lives. It is a rare but wise mother who sees the folly in giving her little girls Barbie dolls and protects their impressionable minds from focusing on dating, achieving an anorexic figure, and dressing like a call girl for the beach or dance. Have you ever been to a wedding where the bridesmaids' dresses made you blush? Or to a fancy restaurant on prom night? It grieves my heart to see so many young girls dressed provocatively and to know of the great loss of innocence that will occur that night. I will never forget the quaint expression of a godly mentor to me when I was a young mom: "Be sure to guard your children against dishonesty and immodesty—for those sins scare away the Holy Spirit."

1. What are some things a wise mother can do to instill godly values in her daughter concerning fashion, diet, and true beauty?

What concepts from 1 Peter 2:9-10 might a mother endeavor to impress on her daughter's heart?

2. What is important to God in a woman, according to 1 Peter 3:3-4?

Though some have interpreted the above to mean we cannot wear jewelry, to be consistent, we would then not be able to wear clothes. Moderation is the point.

3.   Clothing in Scripture is often a metaphor for conduct. What do you learn from each of the following about what clothing is important to God?
    A. Proverbs 31:25a

    B. Colossians 3:12

    C. 1 Timothy 2:9-10

*4. Peter elaborates on the kind of clothing that is precious to God. Describe the "garment" in each of the following verses in chapter 3:
    A. 1 Peter 3:8a

    B. 1 Peter 3:8b

    C. 1 Peter 3:9

    D. 1 Peter 3:10

    E. 1 Peter 3:11

*5. Then he tells us the secret for wearing this kind of clothing in 1 Peter 3:15a. What is it and what does this mean?

In a Christmas sermon, Dr. Bruce Porter said:

Because Jesus came into our world,
we find our strength from another world.
Because Jesus came into our world,
our morals are received from another world.
Because Jesus came into our world,
there is another world in which we sing.[50]

Memory Work
Review 1 Peter 3:4 and begin memorizing 1 Peter 3:5.

Day 2: The Holy Women of Old
Peter tells us if we put our hope in God, if we sanctify Christ in our hearts, then out of the wellspring of the heart will flow the beautiful virtues of purity, humility, gentleness, and quietness. We will then be like Sarah and the holy women of old who put their hope in God. Some say Peter was probably referring to the wives of the two other patriarchs, which would mean Rebekah, the wife of Isaac, and Rachel and Leah, the wives of Jacob. Perhaps, and we will look at a few glimmerings of character in them, but other women seem better choices when describing women who "put their hope in God."

6.   In each of the following explain how the "holy woman of old" exemplified Peter's standards. Then rate yourself on a scale of 1 to 10, on how well you are doing. (1: Not at all! 10: Perfect!)

   A. Purity: Rebekah in Genesis 24:16

   B. Reverence for God: Hannah in 1 Samuel 1:1–2:11

*C. A gentle and quiet spirit: Ruth in Ruth 2

D. Put their hope in God: Leah in Genesis 29:31-35 (Leah and Rachel don't seem to me to have the inner beauty Peter describes, though Leah does mature. How do you see it here?)

*E. Submissive to their own husbands: Sarah in Genesis 18:12

This is the example that Peter uses in 1 Peter 3:6, so it is important that we use the same example concerning Sarah. It is an intriguing example because she's not being particularly respectful in her laughter and in what she says, but as Robert Johnstone discerningly observes in a commentary from 1888: "In speaking to herself, Sarah refers to Abraham as 'my lord,' showing the true way she respected him and thought of him."[51]

In 1 Peter 3:6 we are told Sarah "obeyed" Abraham. This is the only place in a Christian setting where the word *obey* is used in regard to wives. Everywhere else obedience is for children (and children of God) and *submission* is the word used for wives. Submission differs from obedience in that it implies a voluntary cooperation, which certainly seems to be the overall picture of Sarah and Abraham's marriage. In the *Word Biblical Commentary*, J. Ramsey Michaels cautions "not to read too much profound theology into Peter's simple language."[52] And Charles Swindoll writes:

Before your feathers get ruffled by what this says of Sarah ("obeyed"), it will help you to realize the Greek verb means "to pay close attention to" someone. It's the idea of attending to the needs of another. . . .[53]

7. Do you pay close attention to your husband's needs? Does he get priority over the others in your life? Give evidence.

*8. Is the Holy Spirit speaking to you concerning any of the above? If so, how?

9. If a woman blessed with outward beauty does not have inner beauty, what is she like according to Proverbs 11:22?

Day 3: Sarah's Daughters

Peter is encouraging us to be like Sarah, and then, as daughters are often like their mothers, we will be her daughters. It is similar to:

> But I tell you: Love your enemies and pray for those who persecute you, that you may be sons of your Father in heaven. He causes his sun to rise on the evil and the good, and sends rain on the righteous and the unrighteous. (Matthew 5:44-45)

Sarah was a godly woman, a submissive woman, and Josephus said the fame of her beauty and modesty had spread throughout the land.[54] However, she made some big mistakes, as all mortals do. Peter is not urging us to imitate those mistakes! Though that may seem obvious, it needs to be stated. For example, some have taught that if your husband asks you to do something immoral (as Abraham did twice with Sarah), you should submit and trust that God will deliver you in the nick of time (as God did with Sarah). I'll never forget a woman who came to me after she had undergone an abortion at her husband's request. "Dee, why didn't God deliver me in the nick of time?" How angry I felt at the false teaching that led her astray! In *The Glory of Suffering*, Robert B. Deffinbaugh writes:

> I want it to be very clear that I do not embrace the position that women are to imitate Sarah by submitting to every request of her husband, whether sinful or not. As with our submission to others in authority, we must always limit our obedience to those things which do not clearly violate God's commands. Sarah was wrong to participate in the deception that she was Abraham's sister rather than his wife. She should have said, as Peter later would do, "We must obey God rather than men." Wives are to submit to their husbands when they doubt the wisdom of their leadership, but not when they know it requires them to sin.[55]

Read 1 Peter 3:6 carefully.

You are her daughters if you do what is right and do not give way to fear.

*10. In order to be Sarah's daughters, what two things must we be sure to do according to the above?

11. One of the prevailing themes of 1 Peter is to be like our Lord and **do what is right**. Skim the whole letter, looking for passages which have this concept, and summarize the essence of each.

*12. Explain, on the basis of each of the following verses, why it is never right to go along with sin.
   *A. 1 Peter 1:15

   *B. Romans 14:12

   C. Acts 4:18-19

   D. Acts 5:1-11

In addition to supporting Abraham in his deception, there is another incident in which Sarah gave way to fear. Read the account in Genesis 16.

13. What mistake did Sarah make here—and why was it wrong?

Who suffered because of it?

Read Genesis 21:1-20.
14. How does Sarah give glory to God in verses 6-7?

How does her old sin come back to haunt her in verses 8-9?

What does Sarah ask Abraham to do and how does he respond? List everything you discover in verses 10-14.

Why do you think God tells Abraham to submit to Sarah?

How does God look after Hagar and Ishmael?

15. Generally Sarah was a wonderful role model, doing what was right and not giving way to fear. Put yourself in Sarah's shoes in the following situations. How do you think she felt? Why did she trust?
    A. Genesis 12:1-5

B. Genesis 13:7-18

C. Genesis 18:1-6

D. Genesis 22:1-19

*16. Read Hebrews 11:8-19 and explain what Abraham (and we assume, Sarah as well) believed that helped them to live exemplary lives.
   A. v. 10

   B. v. 11

   C. vv. 13-16

   D. vv. 17-19

It amazes me that Abraham believed God would bring Isaac back to life after the sacrifice. What faith! It can be frightening to be married to a spiritual giant unless you too are fully convinced that God is faithful.

*17. Is there an area where you need to better trust God? If so, where?

Memory Work
Review 1 Peter 3:4-5.

Day 4: Do Not Fear What They Fear
Prepare your heart by singing "Surely Goodness and Mercy" (p. 138).

Peter specifically addresses the issue of intimidation. Wives who were married to unsaved husbands were experiencing hostility to the Christian message. Believers in general were experiencing persecution. In order to understand how, in the face of intimidation, a woman might find the strength not to give way to fear (v. 6), we must peek ahead to next week's lesson. What is the secret of confidence? Set apart Christ in our hearts!

In *Pilgrim's Progress*, the pilgrims come upon little Much-Afraid in Doubting Castle. Because she has failed to set her hope in God, life has overwhelmed her.

Much-Afraid

Read the following admonitions in 1 Peter 3 to discover how to respond to intimidation. I have put key phrases in bold.

⁴Instead, it should be that of your inner self, the unfading beauty of a gentle and quiet spirit, which is of great worth in God's sight. ⁵For this is the way the holy women of the past who **put their hope in God** *used to make themselves beautiful. They were submissive to their own husbands, ⁶like Sarah, who obeyed Abraham and called him her master. You are her daughters* **if you do what is right and do not give way to fear. ⁹Do not repay evil with evil or insult with insult, but with blessing,** *because to this you were called so that you may inherit a blessing. ¹⁰For, "Whoever would love life and see good days* **must keep his tongue from evil and his lips from deceitful speech. ¹¹He must turn from evil and do good; he must seek peace and pursue it.** *¹²For the eyes of the Lord are on the righteous and his ears are attentive to their prayer, but the face of the Lord is against those who do evil." ¹³Who is going to harm you if you are eager to do good? ¹⁴But even if you should suffer for what is right, you are blessed.* **"Do not fear what they fear; do not be frightened." ¹⁵But in your hearts set apart Christ as Lord. Always be prepared to give an answer to everyone who asks you to give the reason for the hope that you have. But do this with gentleness and respect,** *¹⁶keeping a clear   conscience, so that those who speak maliciously against your good behavior in Christ may be ashamed of their slander.*

*18. List any common themes you find from the above concerning how to respond to intimidation.

19. In verse 4, when Peter talks about a "gentle" spirit, it means not insisting on one's own rights, not demanding one's own way. A "quiet" spirit has the sense of being calm and peaceful as opposed to restless, rebellious, or insubordinate. Does this describe your spirit? Give evidence.

How is a woman able to have this spirit according to 1 Peter 3:5?

20. In verse 6, when Peter says "do not give way to fear," he is alluding to Proverbs 3:24-26, particularly verse 25. What does that say?

Again, what is the secret to having that kind of confidence? (Proverbs 3:26)

21. Describe the spirit we should have when facing intimidation (1 Peter 3:9-11).

Again, what is the secret to having that kind of spirit? (1 Peter 3:12)

22. In 1 Peter 3:14 the quote, "Do not fear what they fear" is from Isaiah 8:12-14a. What does that say?

Man fears man, but we are to be different because we know man has no ultimate power. Whom are we to fear and what will be the result? (Isaiah 8:13-14a)

"The fear of man" may be not only the fear of what they can do to you, but the fear of losing their favor. How is this seen in John 12:42-43?

Explain how the above kind of fear might cause a wife to make the wrong choice. Give an example that might be applicable for you.

23. What application would the woman who is married to a hostile unbeliever or a carnal believer be able to make from all of the above?

The Christian wife might often experience cruel treatment from an unbelieving husband, but she was not to live in a flutter of excited terror; she was to be calm and quiet, trusting in God.[56]

24. What application would the woman who is sharing her faith with unsaved friends or relatives be able to make from all of the above

Without humility the unconverted person is put off.[57]

Memory Work
Begin memorizing 1 Peter 3:6.

Day 5: An Exemplary Marriage

Though Peter began by addressing the wife who is married to a hostile unbeliever, the introduction of Sarah as an illustration broadens the scope, for she was married to the believer of believers, to Abraham, that spiritual giant who is the father of all who have faith. Their marriage was an exemplary one, and a very unusual one in a day when women were not valued. Their marriage was a wonderful model of mutual submission, of mutual sharing, and of mutual respect. Each loved, cherished, and respected the other and therefore their marriage was an example of harmony. When Abraham left his people and his land to obey God, Sarah went with him, trusting God and supporting her husband. When Sarah asked Abraham to send Hagar away, though it was very difficult for him, he sought God's face and then returned "to do what Sarah requested."

There were times, however, when they were each wrong and it would have been helpful if the partner had not submitted but had said, in love, "I love you, but before God I cannot do that, for I believe it is wrong." That would have been a good thing for Abraham to do when Sarah asked him to sleep with Hagar, and a good thing for Sarah to say when Abraham asked her to deceive the Pharaoh.

Jane Hansen, in *Fashioned for Intimacy*, writes about our responsibility as "coheirs" (1 Peter 3:7) and as "suitable helpers" (Genesis 2:20-24). God expects us as wives to be in prayer about choices and to gently submit our opinions to our husbands. He expects us to gently take a stand when we feel our husband is making a choice that is not honoring to God. And He expects us to share our hearts with our husbands: not to manipulate them, but to be as iron sharpens iron. As women, because of the nurturing nature God gave us, we are generally more open to sharing soul-to-soul than are men, and our husbands may throw up a wall when we try to share with them or probe the depths of their souls. While I have often counseled women that it is unreasonable and inappropriate to expect men to be like women in the way they share, grieve, and comfort—it is also true that we shouldn't withhold our gift of intimacy because their response in the early years of marriage may have been discouraging. Commenting on the phrase "not be afraid with any terror" in 1 Peter 3:6, Hansen writes:

> "Terror" in the original Greek denotes "to scare or frighten" and is perhaps akin to a word that means "to fly away," like a bird that hears a loud noise.
>
> As a woman begins to share her heart with her husband—even if she is gentle and kind—he may immediately become defensive and self-protective. Instinctively he may throw up smoke screens of anger and intimidation. These tactics are an attempt to drive her back so as to protect his inner safety. He wants to keep her away from that inner sanctum where he has been able to hide from his feelings and emotions for many years, probably since childhood. If the woman will stay in relationship, though, stay open and not respond by retreating again into her own inner self-protectiveness, life and healing will eventually begin to come forth.[58]

*25. A good marriage is the ultimate in friendship. What do you learn about the power of a good friendship from the following proverbs?

　*A. Proverbs 20:5

　B. Proverbs 27:9

　*C. Proverbs 27:17

*26. How might you apply the above proverbs so that you will be a better wife? If you are single, so that you will be a better friend?

27. What do you think God would have a wife do if her husband is resistant to sharing soul-to-soul?

> Companions and counselors must search patiently to find the frozen hearts of their friends. But the most common sign of returning to life is that the warmer the love given, the meaner the response. . . .Our loved one built that hiding place precisely to escape pain. Therefore the attack is automatic, to remove the menace before the walls crumble altogether. . . . Husbands, more frequently than wives, often become meaner and meaner the more their wives express love. Just so, the transformation of hearts of stone is not accomplished by distant, safe prayers and well wishings. Hearts of stone can only be melted by persistent, pain-bearing hearts willing to lay themselves down daily, understanding and forgiving every time the quarry turns to attack, until the ice thorn melts.[59]

28. Do you agree or disagree with the above thoughts? Explain.

29. How faithful are you in praying for your husband? How could you be more faithful?

Memory Work
Finish memorizing 1 Peter 3:6.

Day 6: Heirs Together in the Grace of Life
Only the Spirit of God could have caused Peter to make the revolutionary statement that he did to husbands, to see their wives as "coheirs." Stuart Briscoe comments on the term *coheirs*:

> In the days in which Peter was writing, women were still regarded as property, little better than slaves. The New Testament teaching on the place of women must be seen in this context, and we will realize what a positive, liberating effect it had on the women and what joy it could bring to marriage. By insisting that men see women in Christ, marriage was elevated into a new and glorious position, which we

must affirm in our day. Peter insists the husbands see their wives in this light, as inheritors of God's grace.[60]

30. How does God rebuke or caution husbands in the following passages?
   A. Proverbs 5:18-21

   B. Malachi 2:13-16

   C. 1 Peter 3:7

31. What other observations can you make from 1 Peter 3:7? Look for key phrases, reasons, and warnings.

Tradition says that Peter lived out 1 Peter 3:7, encouraging his wife in her ministry. In *Ecclesiastical History*, Eusebius reports that Peter's wife was actively involved in women's ministry and that she and Peter had children.[61]

*32. The key word in 1 Peter 3:7 is *coheirs*. What light does Romans 8:17 shed on this term?

*Do you show reverence for your husband as a coheir in the grace of life? Give evidence.

33. Do you support your husband as a father, as a servant in the Lord's work—in the same way that you desire his support for you? Give evidence.

In *Heirs Together*, Patricia Gundry warns against doing the fathering for your husband, though it may seem like a favor. She shares some advice that a pastor's wife gave to the young wives of men at Talbot Seminary:

> When our children were small, I tried to free my husband as much as I could from home duties so he could do his work unhindered. I wouldn't do that again, if I had it to do over. I think I denied him some of the pleasures of caring for his children, getting to know all those things mothers are there to see.[62]

34. In addition to "coheirs," there are three other interesting phrases in 1 Peter 3:7. The first is: "In the same way." What do you think that means here, in regard to husbands?

Another intriguing phrase is "live together" (or "live with your wives"). Stuart Briscoe writes:

> In contemporary English we sometimes talk about people "living together," but what we really mean is that they share the same bed. Peter's word has the same emphasis and suggests "living together" with particular reference to sexual mutuality, the sharing of bodies which is an integral part of marriage.[63]

35. Although Peter is addressing husbands, we as wives are also to understand the mutuality of the sexual relationship. What do you learn from 1 Corinthians 7:3-5?

How do you think God would have you apply the above to your life?

Under what condition and for what purpose might a couple abstain from sexual relations? (1 Cor. 7:5a)

Finally, consider the phrase: "weaker partner." Read 1 Peter 3:7 in the Phillips paraphrase:

> Similarly, you husbands should try to understand the wives you live with, honoring them as physically weaker yet equally heirs with you of the grace of life. If you don't do this, you will find it impossible to pray properly.

36. How does J.B. Phillips interpret the NIV phrase "weaker partner"?

J. Ramsey Michaels, in the *Word Biblical Commentary*, supports this paraphrase, explaining that the word *partner* or *vessel* in other places means the physical body.[64] Another possibility is that, having just told women to submit, Peter is now telling husbands not to take advantage of their submission to get their own way. As "heirs together" they should be seeking God's will, not their own.

Read 1 Peter 3:7 in the *New Living Translation*:

> In the same way, you husbands must give honor to your wives. Treat her with understanding as you live together. She may be weaker than you are, but she is your equal partner in God's gift of new life. If you don't treat her as you should, your prayers will not be heard.

*37. What warning does Peter give to husbands who fail to "treat their wives in an understanding way"? (1 Peter 3:7b)

*If you are married to a believer, do you pray together? If not, how might you, as a suitable helper, gently initiate prayer?

An easy routine recommended by Luis Palau is to simply, at the close of the day, allow the wife to lift up her concerns while the husband supports her.[65] For example:

> Dee: Father, please anoint me as I am working on 1 Peter.
> Steve: Yes, Lord, give Dee Your wisdom and discernment.
> Dee: And thank You, Lord, for the wonderful way You were with me today.
> Steve: Yes, Lord. Thank You!

Then the husband lifts up his concerns and the wife supports him.

38. What stood out to you from this week's study?

Memory Work
Review 1 Peter 3:4-6.

Prayer Time
Following the model above suggested for husbands and wives, huddle in groups of three or four. Each woman should lift up her own concern and allow her sisters to support her. When there is a pause, the next woman should lift up her concern.

Seven

Set Apart Christ in Your Heart as Lord

It is a sobering to walk through the ruins of the Roman Colosseum, where Christians were thrown to the lions, or to tour the dark, dank catacombs where they hid, and to reflect on Peter's instructions. They died nobly, with gentleness and reverence for God, and the effect was to bring countless others to God. Tertullian wrote: *"The blood of the martyrs is indeed the seed of the church."* [66]

Memory Work

[15]But in your hearts set apart Christ as Lord. Always be prepared to give an answer to everyone who asks you to give the reason for the hope that you have. But do this with gentleness and respect, [16]*keeping a clear conscience, so that those who speak maliciously against your good behavior in Christ may be ashamed of their slander.* [17]*It is better, if it is God's will, to suffer for doing good than for doing evil. (1 Peter 3:15-17)*

Warm-Up

Giving a blessing means, in part, to speak well of someone. Depending on the time your group has, choose one of the following:

A. Brief Blessing: Go around the room, each woman giving a brief blessing to the woman on her right. For example: *I appreciate Julie's unselfishness— it seems like she is always drawing others out in conversation and serving others.*

B. Showers of Blessing: Do the same as above, but after each woman has been blessed, two (at most three!) others may share sentences of blessing about her as well.

Day 1: Like One Big Happy Family

8And now this word to all of you: You should be like one big happy family, full of sympathy toward each other, loving one another with tender hearts and humble minds. 9Don't repay evil for evil. Don't snap back at those who say unkind things about you. Instead, pray for God's help for them, for we are to be kind to others, and God will bless us for it. (1 Peter 3:8-9, TLB)

The Bible compares the body of Christ to a healthy family. My sister and I may exchange hurtful words, but she is my sister, and I will always love her and always be there for her. My mother may tell me I need a face lift, but I'm not going to cross her off my Christmas card list. In the same way, we are to give one another grace in the family of God.

*1. The first phrase Peter uses is "live in harmony with one another." What does this mean?

*What other keys to harmony does he give in verse 8?

Peter comes back to this theme in 1 Peter 4:8. What does that say and what does it mean?

Ethel Barrett tells of a teenager who was always fighting with her mother. After yet another emotional fight, the teenager stormed out, but something made her go back:

My mother was sitting at the kitchen table and her face was all sort of bent out of shape and she was just sitting there with her hands clasped on the table and staring straight ahead. And she looked so sad. She didn't know I was there for a minute, and then I cleared my throat and said it. I said, "Mama, I love you," and it came out sort of strange and I didn't even know my own voice. My mother looked up at me and then she began to cry, with her shoulders shaking and not making any noise. And then it was like some sort of wall was down between us and I was over there by her with my arms around her and I was crying, too. And then we talked a long time and suddenly things that were bugging us about each other didn't seem so awful any more. The important thing was that we really wanted to try to get along.[67]

Is there an application you could make to your life with someone within the family of God? If so, what?

2. How should we respond to evil? (v. 9)

What two reasons are given?

If we respond to evil with good, as Jesus did, we may see unbelievers come into the family of God and "glorify God on the day He visits us."

When Mercy decides to accompany Christiana on her journey,
Mrs. Timorous says: "Well, I see you have a mind to go a-fooling too."

3.Compare the following two passages and find similar phrases:

1 Peter 3:8-9	Romans 12:9-17

4. How might you apply the above admonitions to your life?

Memory Work
Begin memorizing 1 Peter 3:15.

Day 2: Whoever Would Love Life
As a new Christian, like Much-Afraid in *Pilgrim's Progress*, I lacked the confidence to believe God would protect me. The situation that troubled me was my husband's all-night call. Alone in the big city of Seattle, I had many sleepless nights, alert to every noise and shadow. When I told a godly friend, she suggested I pray through Psalm 34, asking God to place an angel in each corner of the bedroom. That was what freed me from Doubting Castle.

Read Psalm 34.
5. Describe the word pictures found in the following verses of Psalm 34.
   A. v. 5

   B. v. 7

C. v. 8

Peter has already alluded to the above verse in 1 Peter 2:3.
  D. vv. 9-10

  E. vv. 11-14

  F. vv. 15-16

6. How is God speaking to your through the above psalm?

The psalmist was speaking of life on earth, but Peter broadens the scope to eternal life, making this passage extremely relevant for believers who are about to face extreme persecution. J. Ramsey Michaels explains, in the *Word Biblical Commentary*, that reinterpretations of Old Testament passages are characteristic of 1 Peter:

> *"Life," which to the psalmist meant a long and happy life on earth, is to Peter the same as "the grace of life" in v. 7—the eternal salvation is the believer's hope. . . . "To see good days" is to see what is now unseen, the glory in store for Christians at that revelation. The language of the psalm is the language of this world, but Peter has made it metaphorical of the world to come.*[68]

Read 1 Peter 3:10-12.
7.   Think about these verses in a setting of persecution: from the mild ridicule of a relative who labels you as a right-wing religious fanatic to the severity of martyrdom. How do they tell you to behave? Be specific.

On what are you to fix your hope in the face of martyrdom?

Memory Work
Continue memorizing 1 Peter 3:15.

Day 3: To Bring to God
Prepare your heart by singing "Chosen Generation" (p. 136).

I am one of three daughters. My older sister Sally led me to Christ when I was a young mother. She and I began to share our new faith enthusiastically with our sister Bonnie, but she seemed increasingly resistant. Twenty-five years passed. One morning I asked God: "Lord, why is there a wall between Bonnie and You?" The Holy Spirit began to do His convicting work on my heart, showing me that there had been times when I had not been quick to hear, slow to speak, and slow to become angry. There had been times when I had taken the bait my sister had thrown out and gotten into arguments about peripheral issues such as abortion, homosexuality, and political candidates. Had I always kept my tongue from evil? Had I always kept myself from deceitful speech? Had I always answered with gentleness and reverence? No. No. No.

Broken, I confessed my sin to God. Then I went to Bonnie and confessed my sin. As I have been obeying the admonitions in 1 Peter, the wall is tumbling between Bonnie and me and between Bonnie and God.

How we react in the face of mild or severe persecution profoundly impacts our persecutors. Our model? Again, it is Jesus. Peter tells us that Jesus died an undeserved death in order to bring us to God (3:18). As we follow in His steps, as we set Him apart in our hearts as Lord, we must be gentle, we must have a clear conscience, and we must be confident of God's care.

In the 20th century there have been more Christians martyred than in all the history of Christendom. Many think that the situation in America is changing as well—and we will soon move from ridicule to persecution. If we must face severe persecution, if we must face martyrdom, may the words of Peter ring in our hearts.

Read of the first Christian martyr in Acts 6:8–7:60.
8. Stephen exemplifies the confidence Peter describes.

A. Describe Stephen in the face of his persecutors in 6:15.

B. In Stephen's sermon, he shows historically how people failed to recognize ones sent by God and persecuted them. What examples does he give? (7:2-50)

C. How does Stephen attempt to awaken them to their sin in 7:51-53?

D. Whom does Stephen see? (7:55-56)

E. Who is among the witnesses? (7:58; 8:1)

F. What does Stephen say as he dies? (7:59-60)

Read 1 Peter 3:13-17.
*9. What admonitions and encouragements does Peter give to us if we face persecution?
    A. v. 13

    B. v. 14

    C. v. 15

D. v. 16

E. v. 17

10. What application could you make from the above?

11. There was a time when Peter was afraid to confront a maidservant and denied that he knew Christ. In the Book of Acts you see a changed man as he confronts the high court. What stands out to you from his sermon and his manner in Acts 2:14-41?

Memory Work

Complete your memorization of 1 Peter 3:15 and ask God to give you an opportunity to share the reason for the hope within you.

Day 4: The Icy Waters of Death

Prepare your heart by singing "Rock of Ages" (p. 137).

The passage you will study today has confounded the wisest of theologians. Martin Luther said of it:

> A wonderful text is this, and a more obscure passage perhaps than any other in the New Testament, so that I do not know for certainty just what Peter means.[69]

Edmund Clowney comments that study of this passage has progressed since Luther's day, but Luther's confession warns against overconfidence.[70] I would also caution you to read carefully at this oasis and to remember a couple of rules for sound biblical interpretation:

> Don't press individual phrases too hard, and don't take them out of context. Peter paints in bold, broad strokes. If you press the details, you could come away from this

passage saying that "baptism saves," which not only goes against all of Scripture, but against Peter's subsequent clarification (see v. 21). Interpret unclear passages in the light of clear passages rather than clear in the light of unclear. Some have interpreted this passage to say Christ preached to those in hell and gave them a second chance to be saved—however, that goes against the clear teaching that we do not get a second chance after death (1 John 5:12; Hebrews 9:27).

There are many intriguing interpretations of 1 Peter 3:18-22, which you can explore in various commentaries. I will give you the one that seems to prevail and that makes the most sense to me.

There is a unifying theme of water in this passage, and water represents both death and life. In *Pilgrim's Progress*, all of the pilgrims must pass through the icy waters of death in order to get to their life in heaven.

Between them and the gate was a deep river, dark and cold, and there was no bridge. At the sight of the river the pilgrims turned pale, and were silent. The two men said, "You must go through, or you will never get to the gate."

"Is there no other way?" they asked.

"Yes," said the men, "but since the foundation of the world only two, Enoch and Elijah, have been permitted to go that way, nor shall any others ever be so permitted until Christ comes again.

Then they accepted the inevitable. Entering the water, Christian began to sink. He cried to his good friend Hopeful, "I sink in deep water; the billows go over my head; all the waves go over me."[71]

"Be of good cheer," said Hopeful, "I feel the bottom and it is good."

Read 1 Peter 3:18-22.

Peter begins with the example of Christ, which shows the theme of death and life. Then he shows how water represents this theme. He looks back to the days of Noah and to those who stubbornly refused to listen to the Spirit of God being preached through Noah. The water of the flood meant death to the disobedient, but that same water meant life to the eight who put their trust in God when it floated the ark that saved them.

Likewise, baptism is meant to symbolize our death to ourselves when we go under the water and living for Christ when we rise from the water. Just as Christ died and was buried, so must we die (to ourselves and at the end of our lives). Just as Christ was raised, so must we live for Him and know that we too will be raised in spiritual bodies after we pass through the icy waters of death.

Read 1 Peter 3:18-22 again.

12. What is the first picture that Peter gives in verse 18?

13. What historical event does he then refer to in verses 19-20? How many people were saved through the water that floated the ark? How many died?

> Noah and his family were delivered from that evil age by the judgment, the waters of the flood. Yet the judgment of the flood was only provisional, and the deliverance of Noah but a prefiguring, or "type," of the final and full salvation of Jesus Christ.[72]

Questions that have puzzled readers are: Who are the spirits in prison? When did Christ preach to them? Clowney continues:

> Christ's Spirit preached through Noah at the time of Noah to those whose disobedience brought eternal condemnation. [Thus they are in the prison of hell.][73]

14. How does the water of baptism symbolize both death and life?

Read 2 Peter 2:4-9.

15. Whom did God not spare? (Find 3 illustrations.)

Whom did He spare? (Find 2 illustrations.)

16. Will God deliver you? Give a Scripture to show the basis for your trust. (One possibility is 1 Peter 2:24.)

Memory Work
Review 1 Peter 3:15. Has God given you an opportunity to share the reason for the hope within you? If not, stay alert!

Day 5: Dead to Sin and Alive to God
Gwen Shamblin's *Weigh-Down Workshop* is being used in churches throughout the world helping people lose weight and keep it off permanently. What secret does she have? She calls it "basic Christianity." All food God has created is good so you can eat anything. However, God created food to satisfy physical rather than emotional or spiritual hunger. So you are only to eat when you are physically hungry and to stop as soon as you are physically satisfied. When you are emotionally or spiritually hungry, you are to turn to God instead of to food. Simple? Yes. Easy? No.

Food for many of us has become a false god in our lives, and letting go of that god is painful. Gwen compares the journey we must make to the journey the Israelites made from Egypt to the Promised Land. They spent forty painful years in the desert while they learned how to run to the true God instead of to false gods for comfort and security. But Gwen keeps telling those taking the workshop that it will be worth it, that one day we will be free. She says: "Because he who has suffered in his body is done with sin." (1 Peter 4:1b)[74]

This is the concept with which Peter begins his fourth chapter. It is similar to Paul's teaching in Romans 6:8-12. As we learn to die to ourselves and live to God, we find increasing strength and confidence until we actually break free of old destructive habits. When I was a young mom, I was addicted to soap operas.

When I became convicted, I struggled for years. Finally I gave them up for a summer—I missed them, and it was a mild form of suffering. But in the fall the pull was much weaker—until finally, the pull was gone. Then I realized the great freedom of not having to find out what was going to happen at 1:30 each day. I had absolutely no desire to turn on the soaps. I was done with that sin! I was free!

Read 1 Peter 4:1-2.
17. What example does Peter begin with in verse 1?

Because Jesus was without sin, the sin He was finished with was ours.

18. What analogy does Peter make to us in verses 1b and 2?

Can you think of a particular area where you had to die to yourself but then eventually experienced freedom? Share to encourage the group.

19. How does Peter give you the picture that this life is a pilgrimage in verse 2?

What kinds of things have we spent enough time doing? (v. 3)

How might friends from our past life respond when we are no longer willing to join them in the things that are not pleasing to God? (v. 4)

What will they have to do? (v. 5)

20. Why has the Gospel been preached throughout the ages? (v. 6)

The Gospel not only saves us from the penalty of sin, but the power of sin.

Read Romans 6:8-12.
21. What is the primary teaching of this passage?

How is this similar to 1 Peter 4:1-6?

Personal Action Assignment
Are you in bondage to a repetitive sin? When the urge comes to speak unkindly, watch a questionable show, overeat, overspend, etc., fall to your knees and ask God to meet your need. Then wait—and see how creative He can be. Waiting is the painful part, but she who suffers (by dying to herself and putting on Christ) can be done with sin. Wouldn't it be wonderful to be set free? Freedom won't come overnight, but you can be set free if you don't give up!

Memory Work
Review 1 Peter 3:15.

Day 6: Time Is Short—Pray Hard!
Whether you are thinking in terms of the second coming of Christ or the end of your life, time is short. If you are young, you may not believe me when I tell you how fleeting your life is—but it is, it is!

I remember longing for my babies to get big enough to crawl, and then to walk, and then to talk—I wished them into adulthood. Especially for the first, I did not realize how short my time was to cherish his childhood and to train him in the way he should go.

It seems just a short time ago that we moved to Nebraska—I, a young woman, full of hopes and dreams. Now seventeen brief years later I am middle-aged, my knees are arthritic, and I am a grandmother. Where did the time go? Did I use those years of strength the best ways I could?

How much more clearly I am understanding, now that I am in my fifties, that I have only one life, that it will soon be past, and that only what is done for Christ will last. This is a pilgrimage—and it will be over before you know it.

How are we to live this fleeting life? Peter closes his letter summarizing his most important admonitions. What is first? Prayer.

Read 1 Peter 4:7.
22. With what statement does Peter open verse 7? What could this mean in regard to the end times, persecution, the recipients of this letter, and us?

23. How does he open the following sentence? What does this mean?

Find similar admonitions in 1 Peter and give the verse references.

Compare this to Ephesians 5:16-17. What similarities do you see?

24. We don't know when Christ will come back or when we will die—but either event could happen at any moment. At each stage of our lives, our opportunities are fleeting. The following opportunities may be past or you may be in the midst of them. Consider:

A. High school and college is a time when our peers are more open to the Gospel than any other time. How well did you use that time?

B. Small children are like wet cement. How well did you love and train your children when they were small? (Your grandchildren?)

C. How well have you honored and loved your parents and grandparents?

D. Consider the gifts God has given you in terms of talents, spiritual gifts, and material resources. How well have you used them?

E. If Christ were to return today, or if you were to die, what important things would be left undone?

25. The most important thing we are to do is to pray. Review what Peter said in:
    A. 1 Peter 3:7

    B. 1 Peter 3:12

    C. 1 Peter 4:7

What hinders the effectiveness of prayer?

Prayer Time
In groups of three or four, if you are physically able, kneel, with your Bibles open on chairs before you. Go through the following exercise.

Praise: One woman reads 1 Peter 1:3-5. Then share sentence prayers of praise to God based on this passage.

Confession: Another woman reads 1 Peter 1:15-16. Take turns confessing where you have fallen short of the holiness of God. After all who will have confessed audibly, take another minute to confess sins silently.

Supplication: Another woman reads 1 Peter 3:12. Then take turns lifting your needs to the Lord. After a woman has lifted her need, one or two others should say sentence prayers to support her.

Closing: The woman who opened should close by reading 1 Peter 4:7 and saying, "In the name of Jesus, Amen." As you rise, hug one another, and if you are not too shy, kiss one another on the cheek with a kiss of love. (1 Peter 5:14)

Eight

Called to His Eternal Glory

*W*e who are called to eternal glory are called to reflect that glory by administering grace as we sojourn through this earth. Pictures of confident women come to my mind:

4:8*Above all, love each other deeply, because love covers over a multitude of sins.*
I see my dear friend who is married to an unbeliever overlooking his gruffness and thoughtlessness because she loves him and desires for him to come to Christ.

4:9*Offer hospitality to one another without grumbling.*
I see my friend Janet serving tea and cookies to international students in her home, practicing English with them, dispensing Christ's love.

4:10*Each one should use whatever gift he has received to serve others, faithfully administering God's grace in its various forms.* 11a*If anyone speaks, he should do it as one speaking the very words of God.*
I visualize Beth Moore teaching on her video, *A Woman's Heart*, speaking with the authority of the Holy Spirit, dispensing the very words of God.

4:11b*If anyone serves, he should do it with the strength God provides, so that in all things God may be praised through Jesus Christ.*
I see my precious daughter-in-law getting up for the sixth time with baby Simeon, soothing him through the colic, drawing on God's strength.

4:14*If you are insulted because of the name of Christ, you are blessed, for the Spirit of glory and of God rests on you.*

In *Daughters of the Church,* Ruth Tucker describes the martyrdom of two:

> *After being stripped and enmeshed in nets, the women were led into the arena. How horrified the people were as they saw that one was a young girl and the other, her breast dripping with milk, had just recently given birth to a child. Consequently, both were recalled and dressed in loosely fitting gowns. Perpetua was tossed first and fell on her back. She sat up, and being more concerned with her sense of modesty than with her pain, covered her thighs with her gown, which had been torn down one side. . . .Noticing that Felicitas was badly bruised, she went out to her, holding out her hands and helping her to her feet. . . . They kissed each other so that their martyrdom would be completely perfected by the rite of the kiss of peace.*[75]

5:5 *Clothe yourselves with humility toward one another, because, "God opposes the proud but gives grace to the humble."*

A young widow cleans for me. Though intelligent and gifted, no job is too humble, no request too demeaning. She serves as unto the Lord.

Memory Work

Memorize 1 Peter 4:8. Extra credit? Do the whole passage below.

8Above all, love each other deeply, because love covers over a multitude of sins. *9Offer hospitality to one another without grumbling. 10Each one should use whatever gift he has received to serve others, faithfully administering God's grace in its various forms.*

Warm-Up

Share one way this small group has dispensed God's grace to you.

Day 1: Called to Dispense God's Grace

Love covers a multitude of sins. If you are irritated with the people around you for little things, then sin in your life is stymieing the flow of God's grace. God's love should flow from us like a river, refreshing others. Peter was also trying to prepare the recipients of his letter for persecution—so it was vital that they be united in love.

*1. What stood out to you from this week's introduction?

Read 1 Peter 4:8-11 in the Phillips paraphrase.

[8]*Above everything else be sure that you have real deep love for each other, remember-ing how love can "cover a multitude of sins."* [9]*Be hospitable to each other without secretly wishing you hadn't got to be!* [10]*Serve one another with the particular gifts God has given each of you, as faithful dispensers of the magnificently varied grace of God.*

*2. What is the primary way to dispense God's grace? (v. 8)

*What do you think Peter means when he says: "Love covers a multitude of sins"?

3. How is this phrase used in Proverbs 10:12? What contrast is given?

When I was in college in my pre-Christ days, I had a roommate for a semester who drove me crazy. Pretty soon I found I couldn't even stand the way she walked across the room. (Poor girl—she certainly wasn't getting any grace from me!) On the other hand, when my dearest friend borrowed my blouse and spilled catsup on it, I easily forgave her, because my love for her covered a multitude of sins.

4. Do you love others so intensely that you can overlook things in love?

If not, what in your life is stymieing the flow of God's grace?

In What's So Amazing about Grace? *Phillip Yancey explains that grace is amazing because it is so costly. It is absolutely free to the recipient, but very costly to the giver.*[76] *We don't want to forgive when we have been hurt, we want the perpetrator to suffer. That's why grace is amazing. That's why grace is not of ourselves. We must get out of the way for God's grace to flow.*

*5. How are we to offer hospitality? (v. 9)

The Greek word for "hospitality" is *philoxenia*, which means loving strangers, or fond of guests. It has to do not only with welcoming others into your home, but also with a whole attitude toward those in need, whether it be the newcomer to your church, an unsaved teen, or a woman needing mentoring. (I cover this intensely in my woman's guide, *The Joy of Hospitality*.)

What are some ways God's grace has been dispensed to you through hospitality?

How you could imitate her (or his) example?

6.   When someone is preaching or teaching on Scripture, what should characterize his or her speech if she is dispensing God's grace? (v. 11a)

*7. How are we to serve? (v. 11b)

We may be tempted to think that the ministry of the word needs special grace, but waiting on tables, collecting money, or caring for the sick is just a matter of rolling up one's sleeves and getting the job done. Not so. If God is to be glorified by ministry in his name, it must be ministry performed in his strength.[77]

How could you apply this specifically to your life?

8. How did you dispense God's grace yesterday?

How could you today?

Memory Work
Begin memorizing 1 Peter 4:8.

Day 2: Called to Suffer for Christ
Prepare your heart by singing "Rock of Ages" (p. 137).

Peter warns: Suffering is coming. In fact, the present participle shows it has already begun. (Be not astonished at this burning among you.)

In *Pilgrim's Progress,* Faithful continually committed his case to the one who judges justly, even in his martyrdom. Soon a chariot came and whisked him into the clouds to the Celestial City.

Read 1 Peter 4:12-19.

*9. How should we not react to suffering? (v. 12)

Whether the suffering is due to persecution or sin in the world, Joni Eareckson Tada insists the Bible teaches:

God hasn't taken his hand off the wheel for thirty seconds.[78]

10. What evidence do you find from the following that suffering must pass through the hand of God?
    A. Exodus 4:11

    B. Lamentations 3:37

    C. Amos 3:7

    How can this possibly be? someone asks.
    Welcome to the world of finite humans pondering an infinite God.[79]

11. Peter has given one answer in 1 Peter 1:7. Review this. What is it?

*12. Differentiate between the two kinds of suffering in 1 Peter 4:13-15.

13. How can we know if we are "participating in the sufferings of Christ"? One way to know is to see if the suffering was like His. What would be some signs according to the following passages? (1 Peter 2:19, 22-23)

14. One reason for suffering is the fact that God is allowing Satan some freedom during our pilgrimage. Of what did Jesus warn Peter in Luke 22:31-32?

Why does Satan have to ask for permission to cause trouble?

Why might God give permission according to this passage in Luke?

15. What was Job's reason for loving God, according to Satan? (Job 1:9-11)

How are Satan's accusations against Job and against God answered when believers suffer willingly for Christ?

What impact does it have on the world?

*16. With whom must judgment begin? (v. 17)

The judgment for believers is not unto condemnation (see 1 Cor. 11:32). It is the fiery trial (1 Peter 1:7) which refines.[80]

How different is the purpose of the fire in God's house from the fire of the last judgment![81]

What are we to do in the midst of suffering? (v. 19)

Memory Work
Continue memorizing 1 Peter 4:8.

Day 3: Called to Lead Humbly Before God
When God grants you a leadership position, whether it is as a Bible study leader, a mother, a speaker, or a recording artist—one thing is clear, you are not to become a dictator or a prima donna. You are not to use your position to take advantage of the weak, but to serve God. When I was a young mother I heard Larry Christenson explain the difference between wrong and right spankings. In wrong spankings, the parent is irritated with a child, grabs him, and whacks him into submission. A right spanking is approached with real regret, not to lord it over the child, but to train the child to walk in the light. The whole attitude is different for there is gentleness, humility, and the fear of God—and the child can sense this difference.[82]

Read 1 Peter 5:1-5.
17. When Peter appeals to the elders, he gives three descriptions of himself. What are they? (v. 1)

*18. What motives in a leader are displeasing to God and why? (vv. 2-3)

*What should be a leader's motive and why? (vv. 2-4)

19. List any leadership positions you have and how you could apply the above. (Take time with this question.)

*20. How does Peter return to his theme of submission? (v. 5)

With what are we to clothe ourselves? (v. 5)

*Be clothed is a remarkable word. It means to put on a certain article of dress worn by slaves above their other clothing. [Like an apron]. . . . Did not Peter's memory go back to that scene in the upper room . . . when the Master had **girded** himself with the towel, and stooped to the slave's task of washing the disciples' feet?*[83]

21. How could you clothe yourself with submission and serve others today?

Memory Work
Complete 1 Peter 4:8.

Day 4: Casting Our Cares on Him
The secret to confidence is to set your hope on God. Satan wants you to concentrate on your earthly cares. Today, begin your personal quiet time by singing the "Cares Chorus" on page 135. Every time Satan tries to distract you from the Word of God with a worry, cast your cares upon the Lord and go back to the Word.

Read 1 Peter 5:6-9.
*22. What command and promise is in verse 6?

How did you see the above in the life of Christ?

How was Peter humbled by Christ after he had said he would never deny Him? (John 18) How was Peter then lifted up? (John 21)

What comfort could the promise of verse 6 bring to persecuted Christians?

Where do you need to humble yourself under the mighty hand of God?

*23. What command and promise are in verse 7?

Peter is quoting from Psalm 55:22. Read Psalm 55 carefully.
24. What particular pain is the psalmist enduring? (vv. 12-14, 20)

Find some phrases which describe the emotions of the psalmist. Give verse references.

Find some phrases which describe the psalmist's solution. Give verse references.

> *Peter is calling for humility in situations of hostility, betrayal, and persecution. Precisely in such situations, Christians are tempted to react in pride . . . [but] Christians can trust the power of the Lord, for his hand is mighty; they can trust the faithfulness of the Lord, for their cares are his concerns.*[84]

*25. Is there a situation where you are being treated unfairly and are tempted to react in pride? What should be your reaction and why?

26. It is often pride that makes us anxious. How can you see this with Martha of Bethany in Luke 10:38-40?

What does Jesus say to her? (Luke 10:41-42)

*27. How is Satan described in 1 Peter 5:8?

How can we defeat Satan by obeying the commands of verses 6-7?

28. The "one thing that is needful" about which Jesus spoke to Martha is to listen and to obey God. How has He spoken to you today?

How will you obey?

Memory Work
Complete 1 Peter 4:8.

Day 5: The God of All Grace

Prepare your heart by singing "Surely Goodness and Mercy" (p. 138).

As Peter began his letter, now he closes it, with a prayer for grace to fill his readers' lives, to build Christlike steadiness and character in their lives, and to give them the confidence that these trials are temporary: ETERNAL GLORY IS JUST AROUND THE CORNER!

Christiana is received at the Celestial City with all of the rejoicing that her husband received earlier.

Read 1 Peter 5:10-14.

*29. The primary theme of 1 Peter and of *Pilgrim's Progress* is summarized in verse 10. What is it?

*30. The phrase which is translated "restore you and make you strong" is the same word that is used to describe the repairing of broken nets. As we persevere in trial, God will repair and bring to completion what is lacking in character. How has God done that in your life during this journey through

1 Peter? (Be as specific as possible.)

31. How does Peter reiterate this message in verse 12b?

32. Why does Peter mention "Babylon"? (v. 13) It could represent Rome, but the interpretation which seems most likely to me is a symbolic one. Look again at 1 Peter 1:1. To whom was this letter addressed?

This group is the new Diaspora—and Babylon was the great city of the world to which God's people were carried captive. Read Daniel 1 and 3. How did godly Jews react to persecution then? What was the secret of their confidence?

33. What is Peter's last statement? (v. 14b) Why, do you think?

Memory Work
Turn to page 133 and review your verses from weeks 1–4.

Day 6: Reflecting on the Journey
Like Mary, the mother of Jesus, godly women ponder God's truths. Today, reflect on our journey.

*34. Without looking at any notes, what do you think your main take-away will be from this study? How will you be applying this to your life?

*35. As you consider the story of *Pilgrim's Progress*, what stood out to you from that? Why?

36. What particular impact has 1 Peter 3:1-6 had on you as a woman?

*37. What have you learned from 1 Peter which will help you with confidence? Be specific.

Memory Work
Turn to pages 133–34 and review your verses from weeks 5–8.

Prayer Time
In groups of not more than six, each woman should lift up her answer to question 34 and two or three others should support her in prayer. Close with the "Cares Chorus."

Memory Verses

³Praise be to the God and Father of our Lord Jesus Christ! In his great mercy he has given us new birth into a living hope through the resurrection of Jesus Christ from the dead, ⁴*and into an inheritance that can never perish, spoil or fade—kept in heaven for you, ⁵who through faith are shielded by God's power until the coming of the salvation that is ready to be revealed in the last time. (1 Peter 1:3-5)*

⁶*In this you greatly rejoice, though now for a little while you may have had to suffer grief in all kinds of trials.* ⁷These have come so that your faith—of greater worth than gold, which perishes even though refined by fire—may be proved genuine and may result in praise, glory and honor when Jesus Christ is revealed. *(1 Peter 1:6-7)*

Chosen Generation

For you are a chosen generation, A royal priesthood, A holy nation, A peculiar people, That you should show forth the praises of Him Who has called you out of darkness, out of darkness, Out of darkness into His marvelous light, Into His marvelous light.

²¹*To this you were called, because Christ suffered for you, leaving you an example, that you should follow in his steps.* ²² *"He committed no sin, and no deceit was found in his mouth."* ²³When they hurled their insults at him, he did not retaliate; when he suffered, he made no threats. Instead, he entrusted himself to him who judges justly. ²⁴*He himself bore our sins in his body on the tree, so that we might die to sins and live for righteousness; by his wounds you have been healed.* ²⁵*For you were like sheep going astray, but now you have returned to the Shepherd and Overseer of your souls. (1 Peter 2:21-25)*

¹*Wives, in the same way be submissive to your husbands so that, if any of them do not believe the word, they may be won over without words by the behavior of their wives,* ²*when they see the purity and reverence of your lives.* ³*Your beauty should not come from outward adornment, such as braided hair and the wearing of gold jewelry and fine clothes.* ⁴Instead, it should be that of your inner self, the unfading beauty of a gentle and quiet spirit, which is of great worth in God's sight. *(1 Peter 3:1-4)*

4Instead, it should be that of your inner self, the unfading beauty of a gentle and quiet spirit, which is of great worth in God's sight. **5For this is the way the holy women of the past who put their hope in God used to make themselves beautiful. They were submissive to their own husbands, 6like Sarah, who obeyed Abraham and called him her master. You are her daughters if you do what is right and do not give way to fear. (1 Peter 3:4-6)**

15But in your hearts set apart Christ as Lord. Always be prepared to give an answer to everyone who asks you to give the reason for the hope that you have, But do this with gentleness and respect, *16keeping a clear conscience, so that those who speak maliciously against your good behavior in Christ may be ashamed of their slander. 17It is better, if it is God's will, to suffer for doing good than for doing evil. (1 Peter 3:15-17)*

8Above all, love each other deeply, because love covers over a multitude of sins. *9Offer hospitality to one another without grumbling. 10Each one should use whatever gift he has received to serve others, faithfully administering God's grace in its various forms. (1 Peter 4:8-10)*

Cares Chorus

KELLY WILLARD

KELLY WILLARD

I cast all my cares up-on You,_____ I
lay all of my bur-dens down at Your feet. And
an - y - time____ that I don't know what____ to do, I will
cast all my cares up - on You._____

179   Chosen Generation

Words and Music by
JEANNIE CLATTENBURG and RICK POWELL

For you are a cho - sen gen - er - a - tion, A roy - al

priest - hood, A ho - ly na - tion, A pe - cul - iar

peo - ple, That you should show forth the prais - es of

Him Who has called you out of dark - ness, out of

dark - ness, Out of dark - ness in - to His mar - vel - ous

light,_____ In - to His mar - vel - ous light.

Rock of Ages

Augustus M. Toplady

Thomas Hastings

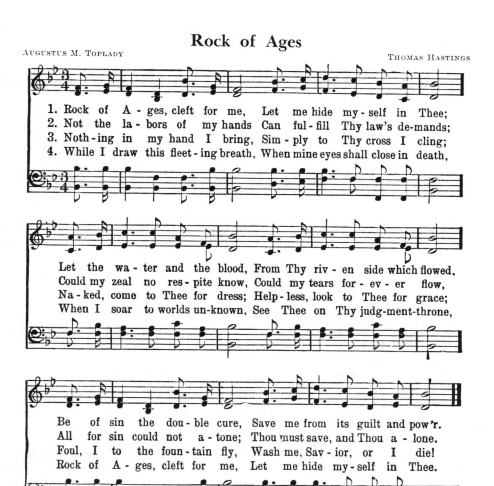

1. Rock of A - ges, cleft for me, Let me hide my - self in Thee;
2. Not the la - bors of my hands Can ful - fill Thy law's de-mands;
3. Noth-ing in my hand I bring, Sim - ply to Thy cross I cling;
4. While I draw this fleet - ing breath, When mine eyes shall close in death,

Let the wa - ter and the blood, From Thy riv - en side which flowed,
Could my zeal no res - pite know, Could my tears for - ev - er flow,
Na - ked, come to Thee for dress; Help - less, look to Thee for grace;
When I soar to worlds un-known, See Thee on Thy judg-ment-throne,

Be of sin the dou - ble cure, Save me from its guilt and pow'r.
All for sin could not a - tone; Thou must save, and Thou a - lone.
Foul, I to the foun - tain fly, Wash me, Sav - ior, or I die!
Rock of A - ges, cleft for me, Let me hide my - self in Thee.

Surely Goodness and Mercy

JOHN W. PETERSON
ALFRED B. SMITH

JOHN W. PETERSON
ALFRED B. SMITH

1. A pil-grim was I and a-wan-d'ring, In the cold night of
2. He re-stor-eth my soul when I'm wea-ry, He giv-eth me
3. When I walk thro' the dark lone-some val-ley, My Sav-ior will

sin I did roam, When Je-sus the kind Shep-herd found me,
strength day by day; He leads me be-side the still wa-ters,
walk with me there; And safe-ly His great hand will lead me

CHORUS

And now I am on my way home.
He guards me each step of the way. Sure-ly good-ness and
To the man-sions He's gone to pre-pare.

mer-cy shall fol-low me All the days, all the days of my

life; Sure-ly good-ness and mer-cy shall fol-low

Surely Goodness and Mercy

★ Opt. D.C. The following section may be reserved for use with final chorus only.

Sources

One: Strangers on Earth

1. Eugene H. Peterson, *The Message: The New Testament in Contemporary English* (Colorado Springs: NavPress, 1993), 486.

2. J. Ramsey Michaels, *Word Biblical Commentary*, eds. David A. Hubbard, Glenn W. Barker and Ralph P. Martin, "1 Peter." Vol. 49 (Dallas: Word, 1988), lv.

3. Warren Wiersbe, *Be Hopeful* (Colorado Springs: Chariot Victor, 1982), 8.

4. R.C. Sproul, speaking at the Christian Booksellers Association International Convention, Dallas, June 1998.

5. Tacitus, as quoted in *1 Peter James: Living through Difficult Times*, Serendipity Group Bible Study (Littleton, Colo.: Serendipity, 1995), 8.

Two: The Purpose of Our Earthly Journey

6. Joni Eareckson Tada and Stephen Estes, *When God Weeps: Why Our Sufferings Matter to the Almighty* (Grand Rapids: Zondervan, 1997), 56.

7. John Bunyan, *The Pilgrim's Progress* (England: Thomas Nelson and Sons Ltd., n.d.), 13–14.

8. Eugene H. Peterson, 487.

9. B.C. Caffin, *The Pulpit Commentary*, eds. H. D. M. Spence and Joseph S. Excell, "1 Peter." Vol. 22. (Peabody, Mass.: Hendrickson, n.d.), 2.

10. John Bunyan, *The Pilgrim's Progress* (New York: Harper Collins, n.d.), 30.

11. Edmund Clowney, 55–57.

12. Dr. Stephen Olford, "The Reality of the Yielded Heart." Cassette tape (Memphis: Encounter Ministries).

13. Ibid.

14. Ibid.

15. John Bunyan, retold by James H. Thomas, *Pilgrim's Progress in Today's English* (Chicago: Moody, 1964), 30.

16. Cynthia Heald, *A Woman's Journey to the Heart of God* (Nashville: Nelson, 1997), 39–42.

Three: Precious, Chosen, and Beloved

17. Edmund Clowney, 85.

18. Beth Moore, *A Woman's Heart: God's Dwelling Place* (Nashville: Lifeway, 1995), 121.

19. John Bunyan, *The Pilgrim's Progress* (Chicago: Covenant Press, 1978), 48.
20. Ibid., 48, 50.

Four: Understanding Submission in the Context of 1 Peter
21. James Slaughter, "Submission of Wives (1 Pet. 3:1a) in the Context of 1 Peter," *Bibliotheca Sacra* 153. January–March 1996, 66.
22. Warren Wiersbe, 58.
23. Harriet Beecher Stowe, *Uncle Tom's Cabin* (New York: Modern Library, 1985), 444–445.
24. B.C. Caffin, 75.
25. Corrie ten Boom with John and Elizabeth Sherrill, *The Hiding Place* (Old Tappan, New Jersey: Fleming, 1971), 176.
26. Edmund Clowney, 127–128.
27. James Slaughter, 64.
28. James Slaughter, "Winning Unbelieving Husbands to Christ (1 Pet. 3:1b-4)," *Bibliotheca Sacra* 153. April–June 1996, 199–200.
29. J.N.D. Kelly, *A Commentary on the Epistle of Peter and Jude* (Grand Rapids: Baker, 1981), 127.
30. J.H.A. Hart, *The Expositor's Greek Testament*, ed. W. Robertson Nicoll, "First Peter." 5 vols. (reprint, Grand Rapids: Eerdmans, 1974), 5:63.

Five: Winsome, Winning Women
31. Kathy Troccoli, *My Life Is in Your Hands* (Grand Rapids: Zondervan, 1997), 39.
32. Ibid., 74–75.
33. John Dawson, as quoted in Cindy Jacobs, *Women of Destiny* (Ventura, Calif.: Regal, 1998), 16.
34. B.C. Caffin, 35.
35. Mary A. Kassian, *Women, Creation and the Fall* (Westchester, Ill.: Crossway, 1990), 74.
36. James Slaughter, "Winning Unbelieving Husbands to Christ (1 Pet. 3:1b-4)," 201.
37. Edmund Clowney, 129.
38. James Slaughter, "Submission of Wives (1 Pet. 3:1a) in the Context of 1 Peter," 71–72.
39. Jo Berry, *Beloved Unbeliever: Loving Your Husband into the Faith* (Grand Rapids: Zondervan, 1981), 11–12.
40. John Bunyan, retold by James H. Thomas, 159–160.
41. Jo Berry, 45.

42. Edmund Clowney, 130.

43. John Bunyan, retold by James H. Thomas, 51.

44. Beth Moore, "New Starts and Barren Hearts." Video tape, (Nashville: Lifeway, 1995).

45. Gordon J. Wenham, *Word Biblical Commentary*, eds. David A. Hubbard, Glenn W. Barker and John D.W. Watts, "Genesis 1-15." vol. 1 (Dallas: Word, 1987), 70.

Six: The Hidden Person of the Heart

46. J. Balsdon, *Roman Women: Their History and Habits* (Westport, Conn.: Greenwood Press, 1962), 240.

47. J. Balsdon, 256.

48. Clement of Alexandria, *Paedagogus* ("Tutor") 3.11.

49. Patricia Gundry, *Heirs Together* (Grand Rapids: Zondervan, 1980), 129.

50. Dr. Bruce Porter, Church of the Palms, Sarasota, Fla. December 20, 1998.

51. Robert Johnstone, *The First Epistle of Peter* (Edinburgh: Clark, 1888; reprint, Minneapolis: James Family, 1978), 205.

52. J. Ramsey Michaels, 165.

53. Charles Swindoll, *Strike the Original Match* (Portland: Multnomah, 1980), 49.

54. Flavius Josephus, "The Antiquities of the Jews." *Josephus: Complete Works.* Trans. by William Whiston (Grand Rapids: Kregel, 1981), 33.

55. Robert B. Deffinbaugh, "The Glory of Suffering: A Study of 1 Peter" (Biblical Studies Press, 1996): Lesson 14, online, Internet, August 22, 1998.

56. B.C. Caffin, 130.

57. Dr. Stephen Olford, "Faith Under Fire." Cassette tape (Memphis: Encounter Ministries).

58. Jane Hansen, *Fashioned for Intimacy* (Ventura, Calif.: Regal, 1997), 91.

59. John and Paula Sandford, *The Transformation of the Inner Man* (South Plainfield, N.J.: Bridge Publishing, Inc., n.d.), 217–218.

60. D. Stuart Briscoe, *When the Going Gets Tough* (Ventura, Calif.: Regal, 1982), 132–133.

61. Darrell L. Bock, Luke, vol. 1. 1:1–9:50 (Grand Rapids: Baker, 1994), 436.

62. Patricia Gundry, 132.

63. D. Stuart Briscoe, 134.

64. J. Ramsey Michaels, 169.

65. Luis Palau, "A Biblical Look at the Family." Cassette tape (Colorado Springs: Focus on the Family, 1984, 1996).

Seven: Set Apart Christ in Your Heart as Lord

66. Tertullian, as quoted in Edmund Clowney, 145.

67. Ethel Barrett, *It Only Hurts When I Laugh* (Glendale, Calif.: Regal, 1973), 152.

68. J. Ramsey Michaels, 180.

69. Martin Luther, as quoted in Edmund Clowney, 156.

70. Edmund Clowney, 156.

71. John Bunyan, retold by James H. Thomas, 151.

72. Edmund Clowney, 164.

73. Ibid.

74. Gwen Shamblin, Weigh-Down Workshop, video series (Franklin, Tenn.: The Weigh-Down Workshop Inc., 1996).

Eight: Called to His Eternal Glory

75. Ruth A. Tucker and Walter L. Liefeld, *Daughters of the Church* (Grand Rapids: Zondervan, 1987), 101–102.

76. Philip Yancey, *What's So Amazing About Grace?* (Grand Rapids: Zondervan, 1997), 100.

77. Edmund Clowney, 186.

78. Joni Eareckson Tada and Kent Estes, 69.

79. Ibid.

80. B.C. Caffin, 176.

81. Edmund Clowney, 195.

82. Larry Christenson, *The Christian Family* (Minneapolis: Bethany Fellowship, 1970), n.p.

83. A. Maclaren, *The Pulpit Commentary*, eds. H.D.M. Spence and Joseph S. Excell, "1 Peter." 219.

84. Edmund Clowney, 211.

Illustration Sources

Pages 4–5, 31: Robert Lawson, *Pilgrim's Progress by John Bunyan* (New York: Harper Collins, n.d.).

Page 9: Guy Wolek.

Pages 11, 32, 51, 60, 123: George Cruikshank, *The Pilgrim's Progress by John Bunyan* (New York: Henry Frowde, 1904).

Page 19: W.S. LaSor, "Peter." *The International Standard Bible Encyclopedia*, vol. 3. eds. Geoffrey W. Bromiley, Roland K. Harrison, and William Sanford Lasor (Grand Rapids: William B. Eerdmans Publishing, 1986).

Pages 22, 111: R.H. Brock, *The Pilgrim's Progress by John Bunyan* (England: Thomas Nelson and Sons Ltd., n.d.).

Pages 28, 130: Randolph J. Klassen, *The Pilgrim's Progress by John Bunyan* (Chicago: Covenant Press, 1978).

Page 72: E.F. Brewtnall, *The Pilgrim's Progress by John Bunyan* (New York: Saalfield, 1905).

Page 85: J. Balsdon, *Roman Women: Their History and Habits* (Westport, Conn.: Greenwood Press, 1962).

Pages 93, 105: F. Barnard, *The Pilgrim's Progress by John Bunyan* (New York: Saalfield, 1905).